AMONG
MOUNTAINS

By the same author:

*St Kilda**
The Royal Mile
*West Highland Landscape**
*Glencoe – Monarch of Glens**
A High and Lonely Place
Discovering the Pentland Hills
Waters of the Wild Swan
*Shetland – Land of the Ocean**

*With photographer Colin Baxter

AMONG MOUNTAINS

JIM CRUMLEY

MAINSTREAM
PUBLISHING

EDINBURGH AND LONDON

First published in Great Britain in 1993 by
MAINSTREAM PUBLISHING COMPANY
(EDINBURGH) LTD
7 Albany Street
Edinburgh EH1 3UG

ISBN 1 85158 544 3

A catalogue record for this book is available from the British
Library

Typeset in Great Britain by Saxon Graphics Ltd, Derby
Printed and bound in Italy by New Interlitho, Milan

To Mike Tomkies

ACKNOWLEDGMENTS

The author would like to thank the following for various forms of assistance and kindness in putting this book together: David Craig, Syd Scroggie, Cameron McNeish, Marion Campbell, and the late Albert Mackie who I thank in spirit. My gratitude to Mike Tomkies goes far beyond the scope of this book, but this is as good a place as any to put it on record.

CONTENTS

'The oldest age with which we have ever rubbed shoulders . . .' – Arkle, Sutherland

Chapter One

A SENSE OF RIGHTNESS

WE WERE NOT present at the birth. We were not there when the mountains emerged from the planetary womb. We did not witness the landscape's birth throes nor the maturing of the mountain mass from infancy to youth to prime, then the crippling, whittling work of the great Ice which shrunk the mass into its agedness, the oldest age with which we have ever rubbed shoulders. It is of no consequence to anything in nature other than ourselves that we have studied geology, glaciation, volcanic upheaval. It matters less still that we have named the rocks and the eras when they were laid down (a curious phrase for such a spectacular throwing up), even christened the very mountains. We were not there.

Because we never saw it, because the reality of what actually happened can never be scrutinised by anything other than the best guesses of our intellect, mountains are beyond us. They stand beyond our comprehension, our grasp of time, and just our grasp.

There are no new mountains, nothing we can nurture or take credit for. We cannot take mountains into our care like an endangered species and nurse them through a captive breeding programme, releasing their offspring back into the wild to give our deserts and oceans, our forests and jungles their soaring dimension. We cannot save mountains. We can only save them from ourselves.

As I write, the fate of a small mountain in the south of the island of Harris is being sealed. To accommodate the largest superquarry in Europe, which will provide the motorways of England and Germany and America with bottoming, a mountain made from the oldest thing we know – Lewissian gneiss 3000 million years old – will be more or less removed. That is what we are capable of. It is not faith we need to move mountains, just commercial expediency and political indifference.

Yet we are not deaf to the mountains' summons. They are such still things, such stupendous stoics, the direct opposite in all our planet's repertoire of ourselves – animated, short-sighted, town-dwelling, creature-comfort creatures that we have become. Mostly, those who answer the summons go to the mountains for fun, to relax, to test their strength, to recharge batteries, to follow tourism's thoughtless advice.

Mostly, we have forgotten how to live in the mountains' midst, and that too puts distance between us and our understanding of the mountain world.

Yet there has always been more to going to the mountains than mere mountaineering, for there is more to the mountain than that particular fluke of geological circumstance which created a chance shape of rock. And there are among us the throwbacks, for whom the mountain world offers however fleetingly a sense, not so much of discovery as of rediscovery. Nothing — no landscape, no set of nature's countless circumstances — so assists the human mind's preoccupation with reaching back, with what we have been and where we came from, nothing . . . so much as the cool embrace of mountain stillness.

I nod my admiration and my agreement each time I read the following sentiment in David Craig's pillar of mountaineering literature, *Native Stones*:

> But when I sit on a six-inch ledge with my feet dangling above a two-hundred-foot drop, the hart's-tongue fern and dwarf hawthorn a few inches from my eyes, the air smelling of moss, wood pigeons clattering out of the tree-tops down below, then at least for a time I have grafted myself back into nature, and the sense of rightness achieved, or regained, is unmistakable.

I have never been much of a sitter on six-inch ledges, but that sense of 'rightness achieved' — and particularly of 'rightness regained' — is one I can lay claim to, for I too have encountered it under other extremes of the mountain experience. Indeed, I believe I may have known the sense of it for longer than I have known mountains.

I cannot now remember the first time I saw a mountain although the chances are it was the Dreish or Mayar, bluntly hunkered bulwarks of my Angus childhood skyline, for their presence if not their exploration was a fixture of car trips out from childhood Dundee into the countryside. But I remember clearly enough the first time that a mountain landscape made a conscious impression on me, aged about ten. Our first family holiday in the Highlands had paused at some unpeopled roadside amid a landscape which looked as though a rock torso was shedding its skin to emerge skeletally naked. Bare rock, gray-black but aglow as any rainbow with white quartz and lichen the colour of canaries (I saw then only the colours, not their meaning, which heightened the miracle) was pushing through heather and bog and mountainside, and I found the sight and scent and the clean feel of it all a marvel. I hugged its 'bleakness' to me (the word was my mother's, uttered as I remember it now, with something of a shudder), experiencing an intensity that sang with wild anthems. An instinct was at work within me which I could not name, and which I was barely aware of then, but which I recognised more than thirty years after the event in David Craig's book.

But if what I felt then for the first time was a sense of rightness regained — and I believe unquestioningly that it was exactly that — then regained from whom? What could a ten-year-old making his first acquaintance with Highland heartlands have acquired, and how could he acquire it by any means other than inheritance?

I scour the obvious sources now and find an infertile field. My father: a soldier, then a telephone engineer who to my knowledge never climbed a mountain, and who rarely expressed an opinion on landscapes except to sigh with a kind of theatrical wistfulness, 'ah, the bonny hills', each and every time he looked at the Fife Lomonds across the Tay from our Dundee tenement window, or the Sidlaw Hills from a roadside, or almost any strikingly lit hills anywhere wherever we encountered them. My mother: Rochdale-born but living in Scotland from early childhood, who seemed to love every rural landscape apart from that pared-to-the-bone place she called bleak. My grandfathers: a Dundee footballer and a north-of-England cinema manager. The latter's claim to wilderness fame seems to have been a passion for bus trips to the Trossachs, a lifelong fascination for the Amazon, and a determination to reach the Falls of Glomach which extended to travelling the last mile on the back of his guide when his weak feet failed him. My grandmothers: one a fine singer with family roots in the Campsies and a distant relative of J.M. Barrie too many times removed to be thoroughly convincing (but from her and my father I inherited the Christian names James Barrie!), the other unknown to me and dead by the time my father was six or seven.

No, I believe – and perhaps this was what David Craig was getting at in those crucial words 'rightness achieved, *or regained*' – that I tread the footprints of older denizens, an earlier mountain order who found not danger and thrills in the mountains but safety and comfort, who walked there confident and attuned. The mountains met their *needs* in a way which escapes us now, in a way which escapes me, except that as my own sense of rightness in the mountain landscape has evolved over the years, the need it meets in me has moved down the mountain: it is being *among* mountains which matters to me now rather than the lure of summits, and that seems closer to the spirit of those older forebears who were the guardians of my mountain inheritance. They were mountaineers for sure, the first truly professional mountaineers: they would have had to be mountaineers for a living, crossing passes and watersheds and judging weather, sheltering beasts in high corries, hunting bird and beast and knowing their ways, prising furtive flowers for their powers and properties and knowing their secret lairs in cranny and boulderfield. They would have had to be conservationists for a living, balancing their own needs against nature's, so that both they and nature thrived, a tricky feat, a lost skill.

It does not follow that I no longer delight in summits nor that I have stopped climbing, but I no longer pursue a mountain merely to pronounce it climbed. Rather the climbing should be a key which unlocks the mountain, and if it opens the way to a corrie ledge smothered in alpine flowers, or an eagle on a carcase, or a conference of mountain hares, or a theatre of the red deer rut, or a ring ousel nest fragrant with stunted juniper, or a new way of looking at something familiar, all these are summit enough for me and likely to consume my attention for hours.

I have no idea how many Munro and Corbett summits I have stood on and I don't care. Turning mountains into something collectable and clubbable has always seemed to me both bizarre and a disappointing response in a human breast to the mountain

'Nothing so assists the human mind's preoccupation with reaching back so much as the cool embrace of mountain stillness' – Sunrise, Knoydart

superlative. There are a handful of mountains and mountain landscapes to which I return addictively like an unrequited lover craving favours, secrets, intimacies. I think:

What has it been like to be this mountain, to be *so old*, to have watched the rise and fall of the wolf, the spread and the shrinkage of birch and pine forest, the cropping devastation of sheep and deer, the deepening indelibility of man's stamp, to see all of that as so much transience, yet to be buoyed up or wounded at every advance and retreat of nature?

Aldo Leopold, whose *Sand County Almanac* is possibly the greatest work of nature writing ever, wrote:

> I now suspect that just as a deer herd lives in mortal fear of its wolves, so does a mountain live in mortal fear of its deer. And perhaps with better cause, for while a buck pulled down by wolves can be replaced in two or three years, a range pulled down by too many deer may fail of replacement in as many decades.

How much truer is that sentiment in Scotland where our mountains have been wolfless in as many centuries, where the wolf has been supplanted by agricultural and sporting regimes as contemptuous of mountains as their perpetrators' ancestors were contemptuous of wolves. Leopold wrote that 'Only the mountain has lived long

'It is being among *mountains which matters to me now'* . . . — *Bla Bheinn, Skye*

'Everyone who climbs should go alone, at least once . . .' — *Brocken spectre, Beinn Sgritheall*

enough to listen objectively to the howl of the wolf.' In Scotland, only the mountain has lived long enough to listen objectively to the wolfless quietude.

So I sit high on a favourite mountain, on the rim of a corrie 500 feet above the treeline, and I listen to the mountain and I hear the wolf. But Leopold was right: only the mountain has lived long enough to listen objectively to the howl of the wolf, to give it meaning, to mourn its passing as an aged mother might mourn the death of the son she outlived from the unique perspective of the one who also remembers how she gave him life.

In such places I feel the need to try and win the mountain's confidence, to establish the benevolent purpose behind my presence in the mind of the mountain. The Scot on his native heath values a moral freedom to roam and claims it for his birthright. So he should, but it is nothing more than a self-important and hollow arrogance if he will not acknowledge its subservience to nature's laws.

Am I *fit* to be here?

Fit company for mountains?

Suitably respectful of where I am? This matters. The answers to such questions must always be deceptions of a kind, for the true answer is no: every step taken by every human on a mountain is a step feared by the life which inhabits the mountain, and as the exterminator of the wolf, a step reviled by the mountain. We go because we are drawn there. I think we should improve the quality of our going. Who pauses often in the early stages of a mountain trek to test the mountain embrace and watch it grow, to contemplate what the mountain has to offer, to consider what might be offered in return? For it is a crude dismissal of the mountain's vast hospitality to go empty-handed. Climbing in a club or a party is not good for the quality of the going. Everyone who climbs should go alone, at least once, even if all they do is walk a low mile among mountains and sit and listen, for the quality of the going will outlast every mob-handed expedition they ever make.

In sifting this book from my own mountain years, I have purposely dwelled on those mountains which have made impressions on my life I will never shake off, mountains whose company I have kept many times and without leaving a trace of my passing, because that is the highest compliment we can pay them. Whatever we, as a species, do among mountains, whether we climb them, study them, seek out their secrets, own them, make a living from them, manage them, play on them, write about them, paint them or turn them into symphonies . . . if we can all do it so that as individuals we leave no trace of our passing, then the mountains will have no problems to deal with other than the problems of simply being mountains, and we will spare ourselves the problems caused by the fact that we have caused the mountains problems.

The bagger of peaks may scoff at all this, which is his privilege, but I would ask him to go back to a group of peaks he has already bagged, to dwell not on their summits but among their silences, to sit and listen, and see if he cannot hear the wolf or an older footfall, see if he cannot perceive, however fleetingly, a sense of rightness regained.

Chapter Two

STEPS IN THE RIGHT DIRECTION

A LARK BOUNCES down the warm air, carelessly spilling song. A child's eye is held in thrall by its stringless yo-yo. Then – that climactic commitment of the flight when the song silences, the bird folds to a fast, free curve and a tussocky thud. The child gasps. The bird has fallen!

There is a smatter of sound by the frontier of thrusting oats. The lie of the ground shows the child that the lark is not only unhurt but running, now standing, and where it stands a tussock parts to permit the cautious step of a second bird. The child revises his opinion. *This* is the bird which fell. See how it trails a broken wing!

The child stands (he has been sitting on a football, waiting, but no one came to play), advances to see better. He has not yet learned the craft of stillness, and sees nothing. The larks have chameleoned into a bewilderment of grasses, led by the broken-winged one, which, curiously, is still deft enough to elude the child. By the time he unravels the moment's beguiling secret and the broken wing has miraculously healed itself, the child has found his first nest. Into these grass rags have been sewn riches, a silk purse fashioned from the sow's ear of the field's chaff and litter, an oyster of left-overs with four blotched pearls.

In the following weeks, the pearls crack and cradle four impossibly ugly non-larks; these fatten and fledge and fly impossibly lark-like. The nest stills. Ragged fragments of its walls stir in the spring-into-summer winds. The child's field-edge football concedes to cricket. Then, one early summer hour he stumbles on the nest again and finds three new pearls. A lark scuttles away through the tussocks trailing a wing. It has all begun again.

But now the effect on the child changes. A thought lodges in his mind to make a wretched misery of his nights. All this has happened out in the field *on its own*. How can such tiny birds survive all night in the field on their own? Surely they are afraid? Surely they must be looked after? Perhaps some Wee Willie Winkie of the wilds goes soft-shoed through the fields in the eerie half-light of these darkless northern nights, soothing and guarding? Night after night the birds' plight invades and troubles his dreams. Yet every day after every night, there they are, as right as summer rain. Every

day after every night, a bit more of the miracle has unfolded. Small reassurances begin to root in the child's mind, the bad dreams fade. He realises slowly that the field offers the birds all they need, all that it takes to succour the miracle, and as yet he knows nothing of the hawk which can pluck the lark from the top of his thin column of song. It is out there, this miracle, it is on its own, and it works. It is wild. It is the wildness of it all which will impress the child and hatch within him . . .

. . . All the way up to Coire an Lochain of Braeriach in the highest Cairngorms, the wind hews a tunnel of hammering air across the mountain. The child-turned-man has been blown off his feet fourteen times, once on to a snow slope which scoops him 200 feet back down the mountain but leaving him no worse than bruised and breathless. Finally he wins into the corrie, ears pained by the ceaseless windsong. There he unsettles two ptarmigan. He who has been granted all the consideration of a November leaf by the wind now watches the ptarmigan burrow unflinchingly into its path, confidently deflecting the banshee. Wind and birds are wild kin of the same landscape and understand each other. The wind permits the birds safe passage. He watches them land and in the instant of landing they are snow-and-stone in a land of snow-and-stone. In that instant too, the man's wind-numbed mind resurrects the undimmed image and the memory of the chameleon larks, for theirs was the Angus field of my own nursery years, the Cairngorms the summit of my graduation in wildness. It is wildness which unites lark and ptarmigan in the mind of the child-turned-man. Wildness began to matter to me on the grubby knees of the thwarted footballer, aged seven. Wildness has mattered to me ever since, wild in the sense of those spirits and inclinations of nature and landscape which flourish of their own accord, beyond the reach of man's hand, beyond his scope save for his admiring glance and the finer qualities of his enquiring mind, the finest of which is a wide-eyed childish wonder.

Wildness is a fragile and virtuous thing. It is priceless not just for what it teaches us, not just for the ennobling characteristics with which it can endow susceptible mortals, but for its own sake. Wildness matters because it matters. It is a paradox of the human character that although as a species we have long since set our face against wildness and snuffed the candle of instincts which once burned within us shedding intimate light on the natural world, we can still as individuals throw a smile and a second glance after the free flight of birds, the strut of a stag, the storm-dance of a rainbow. There is a great truth, still, in the sentiment of Gavin Maxwell's foreword to *Ring of Bright Water*:

> For I am convinced that man has suffered by his separation from the soil and from the other living creatures of the world; the evolution of his intellect has outrun his needs as

PREVIOUS PAGE: 'In that mercifully benevolent Angus hill tradition it will always be The Dreish'

18

>   an animal, and as yet he must still, for security, look long at some portion of the earth
>   as it was before he tampered with it.

A tiny fragment of whiteness catches my eye in the sparse heather of the high Cairngorms. It is a ptarmigan feather lodged on a heather stem. It jigs in time to the wind's flailing of the stem, but 90 mph gusts cannot prise it free. I kneel and cup my hands round it to study its tiny tenacity. For that moment, the child is back on his grubby knees seeking out the secrets of wildness. We have yet to learn to snuff the candle of childish wide-eyed wonder. We have yet to learn how to tamper with rainbows. For as long as we do not learn these things, there is hope for wildness.

It was a providential beginning. To reach the lark's field I had to walk up a narrow lane between fields. It was called Elmwood Road (still is, but now it is a suburban street through a rampage of bungalows which began while I still lived there and has scarcely paused for breath ever since, and the city of Dundee has consumed a great deal more of that which was once rural Angus); it climbed to a low crest from which nothing could deflect your gaze away from the summer-blue Sidlaws, the northern barricade of low hills which buttresses the city and its in-bye farms from wilder worlds beyond. If you are destined to go among mountains there will be, somewhere unsuspecting, a step or two in the right direction which will seal your fate for life. For me, it was the few hundred yards from the football-cricket pitch to the top of the fields, for such a walk went north and the closed, safe world fell away to the incomprehensible miles-off hill skylines. One way or another, my walking and climbing has had a northern bias ever since. Crucially, those first few unwitting steps to the top of the field followed the footsteps of a well-worn tradition, for they would lead to an apprenticeship in the Sidlaws, to paying my dues among the higher hills of the Angus Glens (unseen from the field but spread-eagled before you from the Sidlaws), to a traverse of a matchless mountain highway called Jock's Road which would deposit me in turn gasping at the feet of the Cairngorms. It was not just a straight northerly progression, it was a progression in the greatness of mountains, and it ensured that when finally I contemplated the Cairngorms I was as prepared as I would ever be, by the apprentice years, by the casual gossip of my mountaineering elders and betters, by their own fearsome legend.

Somewhere between the lark's field and my first bike trip out from Dundee to the Sidlaws, aged about thirteen, there had been the first Highland holiday. The three cemented into place the foundation stone of a life among mountains. It was a short bike ride, as I remember it. I packed a lunch at breakfast time, set off for the day, and was home by lunch-time having eaten lunch for elevenses. Back in Dundee, my mother was aghast as I staked a claim to a second lunch and wondered where I could go for the afternoon. But a seed had rooted, and however briefly, I had set foot on the holy ground, set in motion a chain of events which remains strong and unbroken more than thirty years later. The next time I went I knew the way, and went singing up Craigowl amid the tall columns of larksong. Craigowl is the highest if far from the bonniest of the Sidlaws. You see its relationship to the city best from the high south end of the Tay Road Bridge where it forms the centrepiece of a slung barrier pinning Dundee to its shore, shielding it from wilder lands beyond. By the time you have reached the city at the north end of the bridge, its own hills have reared up before you and there is no Craigowl. But in your mind's eye you remember its dark and careless crouch, symbol of that other world to which my native city was reluctantly yoked. My confidence on the hill grew as I grew, and through my teenage years, Craigowl, Baludderon Hill and Auchterhouse Hill were all the world I needed, and when I paused on their summits and shoulders to look north, it was only to question the sanity of those who rushed through weekend dawns to the incomprehensible heaps of summits beyond Strathmore. Who could want more than these rumpled friendly hills? The folk you met up here seemed hewn from the same rumpled friendly stuff, and had been climbing these hills forever. This was the barrier aspect of the Sidlaws. Later I would learn to understand them not as a barrier but as a key, one which made those heaps of summits to the north comprehensible. But first I had to learn my hill-going trade, and I wish that good tradition still prevailed. Outdoor education thrust into a school syllabus like algebra is no substitute. There is a limit to what you can learn and feel in a minibus-full of orange cagoules. But go quietly and curiously, dressed in the colours of the hill, and the learning and the feeling are limitless.

So the Sidlaws came into my reckoning, and I owe them everything. Learn to climb them, to walk and wander in them, to find your way about them by your own hesitant efforts and mistakes, the way the burns fall, the lie of the hills' secret folded-away fertile valleys where a kestrel dances down a fast air and flies slow with lowered undercarriage to a raucous and whitened ledge on an old worked-out quarry face, the taloned vole still warm as its small flesh is shared out among a brood of three. Learn the ridgey significance of finely sculpted miniature landscapes pock-marked with hill fort and standing stone and marvel at those ancient hands which fashioned the very hilltops for a living. See the hills as the last petrified wave of the land before it broke on the shores of sea and firth . . . learn all that and you are ready to cross the great divide of Strathmore to that storm-and-snow horizon of the glens, but know that however high and wide your horizons grow you will never tire of the small home hills where a seed rooted.

Countless generations of Dundee people know the feeling, and those Angus places where hill chiels gather are rich in story and fable. One of the best Sidlaw stories was told to me by Syd Scroggie, Dundee's rightly famed blind and one-legged climber-poet. He once responded to a letter of mine thus:

Dear Jimmy,

There's naethin wrang wi the Seedlies, foxes, white hares, the occasional buzzard, and if you can't get a sense of the hills around Craigowl, White Tap and Baludderon Hill then you're wasting your time messing about on Mont Blanc, Aconcgua and Kanchenjunga. John Ireland, a Dundee worthy, had climbed the Sidlaws for seventy

The Angus fields of the author's childhood and their 'northern barricade of low hills'

'I come back to Clova to restore in my own mind who I am and what I stand for'

years unmolested when one day his way was barred by a parvenu farmer. John and his pals could go no further, he said, because this was his land. John pushed past him. 'There's a richt o' wey ower here,' he said, 'gaein back tae the Vehkings.' The farmer played his last card. 'I've got wild horses up there on the hill,' he said, 'and they'll kick you to death.' John does not appear to have been impressed. 'Laddie,' he retorted, 'when furst Eh cam tae they hulls thir wis lions and tigers there . . .'

There is much more in that vein round a pub fire in Glen Clova up by in the Angus glens, and I would have to own up that if I grew up and swilled the first intoxicating hill brew in the Sidlaws, I came of age and first tasted the single malt of it all in Clova. I remember listening to the folk I knew who frequented such places, envied the way the great hill names tripped off the tongue with a casual familiarity . . . Mayar, Craigmellon, Broad Cairn (and Lochnagar was uncontemplatably exotic) . . . but there was one which intrigued more than all the others because it had not just a name but a definite article. Maps may disagree, but to all of us who grew up into that mercifully benevolent Angus hill tradition, it will always be The Dreish. It was on a blunt prow of that inestimable mountain, on a pungent purple day in 1980 that I heard my father's voice in my ear, five years after he died, that fond familiar refrain with which he inevitably contemplated any hillside anywhere: 'Ah, the bonnie hills.' The easy wind that blew that day peeled away the years with the morning cloud, so that the very wind itself felt like a familiar friend.

I mind you, young wind,
the keen clasp of neighbourly Highlandness
and scented berry-breath cool
on Clova's brow. (Those were
my hill-cradling days
daring north beyond Craigowl
and other safe-apprenticed Sidlaws.)

Muckle and mild winds,
west and wild winds,
soft and ice-styled winds
I climbed among since then. Yet

something in this reunion
rings truer than other airs,
harks back and back
to old mountain simplicities
which lay the far side
of care's conniving boulderfield.

I mind you, Angus wind,
you freed my understanding
of Faither's understated sigh
— 'The bonnie hills' —

You should be here, Faither,
not loitering heavenly high
above the Dreish and Mayar
for this one unearthly hour.

Roots go deep in one so thirled to the land. I found my 'idea called home' far from here on the Beallach an Dubh Chorein, and pressed to cough up a top ten of favourite mountains or mountain landscapes (not at all the same thing), I'm not sure that the gathering around Milton of Clova would have crept into the list. And yet. So often with Angus there is an 'and yet'. And yet, whenever I haunt my oldest mountain footsteps and stir my earliest mountain memories I have to acknowledge that between Clova and Glen Doll and that great fork of peaks from the Dreish to Broad Cairn and Craig Mellon, all their corries and lochs and passes and that miles-wide offshoot that goes trundling under the sky over the Capel Mounth, I encounter unfailingly a set of circumstances which push me deeper into myself than elsewhere. I am more tellingly aware here, too, of the debt my life owes to the mountain landscape than elsewhere. It may be that there is one mountain landscape which moves me more, but that too is umbilically secured to Clova, for it lies at the further end of Jock's Road. The Cairngorms will always be the promised land, the ultimate horizon for my own peculiar re-working of that tradition into which I was born and grew willingly. There are many others of the tradition who look no further than the Clova hills, and certainly there was a time in my mountain life when the Dreish was the hub of my world, and Jock's Road and the Capel track fickle spokes which trailed off unreliably to other lands. But there would come a day on the Dreish, strolling hands-in-pooches, April-blissful for Mayar, my mountains awash with spring sun and plover-sigh, when I watched an incomprehensible storm in the far north-west fall on the familiar shapes of the distant Cairngorms, then rip itself from them leaving them the only white mountains in the land. It seemed to me then that in the Cairngorms other forces held sway, greater forces contemptuous of seasons, nature unrestrained.

All this came back to me, twenty-five years or so after I had first crossed Jock's Road for Braemar and the Lairig Ghru and that undreamed-of scale of a mountain realm. I was back in the Clova of my youth, lurching between teens and twenties and forties, donning and doffing the decades like jackets, slip-sliding through my life 'the far side of care's conniving boulderfield' and the other regrettable side too. I was trudging up the Capel track, pausing often to watch slashes of fast, sleet-and-sun squalls which hurtled down from Jock's Road blurring the great corries of the Dreish. I thought of all that had gone on, all that had gone wrong, all that had propelled me and hampered me over my own watersheds and boulderfields. That singular summit at the

The Capel Mounth track, celebrated in poem, graced by a rainbow

Broad Cairn and Loch Muick, lynch-pin landscape of the hills around and above Glen Clova

centre of my thoughts has been the one utter constant of all these years, the one great unchangeable. It had been the first mountain I had ever seen, the first one I had ever climbed, the first one that ever frightened me, the first one I ever slept out on. Yet I had never, until now, felt close to it, drawn to it with something other than a mountaineer's relish.

A particularly turbulent squall smashed down the glen. I watched it come and go, fudge the mountain's shape then restore it, backlit and rimmed by a sudden white blaze of sun. A persuasive man might have approached me then and there and convinced me that on that summit dwelt a species of mountain god. Such gods as I hold to dwell in such places, or at least my idea of them, is glimpsed among mountains at their most seductive. Because the Clova hills (these days at least) bring out the contemplative in me (and because that fact in turn stems from the fact that Clova is where my mountainness comes from, its native heath), I have come to think of them as a set-aside place. For that matter, it is a place where I set myself aside, and therefore, not a place which I seek out lightly, not any more. That is, I concede, a pity, for it is a landscape as well-versed in hilarities and fellowship, hill-fellows-well-met, as it is in sombre solitudes. But in the too recent past I lost my mother, and in the too distant past my father, and because Clova is where the part of me that matters comes from, it is perhaps here that I remember them best, or here that I like to remember them best. Whatever, the mountain-ness of the place commands a unique affection in any roll-call of landscapes. I have always thought of the Cairngorms as the place where I am most at ease with nature and with myself; of Skye as my soul country; of the Buachaille Etive Mor as mountain Scotland epitomised and encapsulated; of Ben Ledi as a friend among mountains; of An Teallach as a superstar among mountains; of Bla Bheinn as the most beautiful of mountains . . . yet I come back to Clova to restore in my own mind who I am and what I stand for.

So I took the Capel track on a vigorous mid-March morning with the mountains braided and badged with old snow, and stopped often to look at my mountain over my shoulder, and as I climbed the curving zig-zags above the forest, Craig Mellon locked itself into place in the landscape wearing a perfect down-curving rim of brilliant snow, graceful and slender as a curlew bill, and I started turning to watch that instead.

In that sporadic fashion I hauled slowly up the track, and as I climbed I began to feel again that old sense of anticipation which presages that moment when you break over the crest of the high moorland shelf and find Lochnagar there. Nothing prepares you for it, for you never know how you will find it. The first time, alone and unwarned, I met the mountain in its own rage of storms, but with the wondrous Meikle Pap standing clear of the storm like a dark lighthouse warning me not to approach too close. I stuck to the track that day and marvelled my way to Loch Muick. I doubt if I took my eyes off Lochnagar until I turned for home. Through the homeward miles, I remember the sense of the mountain following me. A few years later climbing up on to the Moine Mhor from Glenfeshie in the Cairngorms I reached that point when you break over the edge of the plateau miles and find Cairn Toul there.

The scope and scale of it were all that were different, and as my jaw dropped my mind lurched back to Lochnagar and the Capel Mounth.

Now I climbed again, and as I climbed, my old familiar sense of anticipation began to impose itself on a day which had begun with a rhythmic snatch of a poem gnawing away at my mind. It was a snatch, and it gnawed, because I couldn't get it past the second line. It was the work of Syd Scroggie, and what I could pin down of it was just this:

> I will attempt the Capel track
> Old, stiff and retrograde

The lines had got fastened to each other at both ends in my head, so that they came round again and again like a conveyor belt, and although it's a fine opening to a fine poem, there's a limit to how long you can admire two lines of anything without craving the arrival of the third line. On I zigged and zagged, and with each zig I heard 'I will attempt the Capel track' and with every zag there was 'Old, stiff and retrograde'. The thing got so ingrained in my footfall that I stopped to scan the track more than once to see if old Syd himself was somewhere above or below me, but the world was mine and mine alone. The last crest grew close, and I hurried forward, breaking the rhythm and giving the anticipatory urge its head. For once, though, it was not Lochnagar which stopped me in my tracks. The mountain was black and shrouded, unfathomable, unrecognisable, stupendously indefinable, stormbound and lost. But far Conachcraig stood clear of the mass, the moor lay wide and pale gold, and stitching the moor to that far, dark hill in a low-slung weave of colours was the arc of a rainbow. The unexpectedness of it stopped me dead. I had been anticipating a mountain. It was as though it had been removed in the landscape and replaced by a rainbow. Nature as scene-shifter.

And as I stood watching in wonder at the trick which nature had worked, Syd Scroggie's verse materialised and I spoke it aloud to nobody:

> I will attempt the Capel track
> Old, stiff and retrograde
> And get some pal to shove me on
> Should resolution fade,
> For I must see black Meikle Pap
> Against a starry sky
> And watch the dawn from Lochnagar
> Once more before I die.

All the way out to Loch Muick, the rainbow stayed before me while the base of Lochnagar glowered bleakly at the moor, at the storm-wars of its summits, and I went breezily north, pleased I was having the high moor of the day rather than the high mountain of it. Wind and rain stalked the track with me, but light and airy stuff, shot through with sun. My season was spring; the mountain's direst winter.

I took to the Black Hill above Loch Muick, an old haunt, the perfect mountain watcher's stance to admire the set-piece spectacle of Lochnagar. I collect such places, nature's grandstands. The one place from which you cannot admire a great mountain is on the mountain itself. So I number among my beaten paths such unsung places as the Black Hill, as Beinn a' Chrulaiste which contemplates the Buachaille, Carn Elrig in the Cairngorms for its side-long glances into the Lairig Ghru and its head-on, two-eyed view to Braeriach, the little tilted wedding cake of Dun Mor which stares (fearfully it seems) into the Prison of Skye's Quiraing, and Beinn Bhreac on Soay, the ultimate Cuillin-watcher's pedestal.

The Black Hill is a low knob on the moor, a mountainous molehill, but for the effort of sclaffing up the extra four or five hundred feet it swells above the moor, your horizons widen impressively. It is nothing more than a chip off that old block of hills which hems in the north side of Clova, but the fact that at some point in the last great upheaval of what we now call Angus it lurched free of its brethren, confers an airy pedestal status on its broad back. Lochnagar and Broad Cairn and that whole southering horseshoe down as far as Mayar are perfect from here, and if you can contrive a night out and an early summer sunrise here, you win the privilege known to few of seeing them lit with the sun low in the north-east. I made a midsummer night of it once, and the curlew and the golden plover cried through the darkless night, and the orangey monster which rose beyond Mount Keen was unlike any other sun I ever saw heave above any other horizon. Twenty years ago, possibly more, and all I remember is the night and the dawn and nothing of the daylight which followed. Lochnagar burned while Mount Keen smouldered and my Black Hill glowed like hot coals at my feet. A perfect collar of cloud hung round the neck of Meikle Pap, smoke-gray until the sun touched it. For perhaps five minutes it seemed to capture and concentrate the sun's every mote of energy, burning with a barely credible red intensity. Then it vanished, the rock stood unadorned, and the redness paled and threw its diluted fire across the whole mountain mass. To have been there, borne witness to it, then turned for home through the lightening morning with something of the cloudfire in your head . . . such is the stuff of my mind's store at the sound of the word 'Clova'.

When I'm 'old, stiff and retrograde' myself, I will still remember that cloud, the dawn on the Capel track, the debt I owe to an unenigmatic little swelling on the moor called Black Hill, the poem freed by the rainbow, and the wholly admirable spirit of Syd Scroggie, the poet who is himself a part of the magical inheritance we Dundonians call 'goin' up the Clovy'. That poem of his, which he calls 'Ante Mortem', concludes thus:

> And if I do not make the top
> Then sit me on a stone
> Some lichen'd rock amongst the screes
> And leave me there alone,
> Yes leave me there alone to hear
> Where spout and buttress are
> The breeze that stirs the little loch
> On silent Lochnagar.

Chapter Three

THE THREE WINDS

tract *trakt*, n. a stretch or extent of space or time
Chambers 20th Century Dictionary

WE HAVE ONLY one true mountain *tract* in Scotland, the high Arctic plateau land of the Cairngorms, where space and time co-exist vastly.

Its scale confounds.

Its deceptions kill: the fatal tendency is to underestimate.

Its winds kill: tracts of winds as Arctic as the terrain and the scale can ambush you, leaping out from behind the smoke-screen of a breeze. When I think of winds in the Cairngorms, I think of three winds in particular.

The first wind *was* an ambush. I can say in defence of the ambushed that I was young and foolish and among fools. Four fools, then, stomped through the June pinewoods of Rothiemurchus and on into Gleann Einich in crudely high spirits. We were one genuinely experienced mountaineer, one bluffer and two eager trampers (of which I was one) on the point of graduating from our apprentice years. I had already made two long treks into the Deeside Cairngorms, but neither of them had tangled seriously with the mountains' moody extremes. Gleann Einich was my baptism into the Cairngorms through their Speyside portal. The glen that day was a doddle, warm with light showers for our cooling comfort, tangy and fine, and I was fit and twenty. I was also wholly deceived.

We made Loch Einich in good time and discussed camping there. The prospect entranced me. Two for camping, two for going on, including the Mountaineer who held sway, being senior to the rest of us in every respect. I looked longingly at the green and heather-pungent shore, the small beach, the flicker of sandpipers whose calls chuckled and yikkered across the quiet waters. I had in my mind's eye a vision of swimming out into mid-loch, and studying the mountain walls which clasp three of Loch Einich's shores while lying on my back. I wanted to pause and taste it all, to sleep and wake in its midst. Going on could wait until tomorrow. Besides, go on? Go on where? The briefest consideration of the question offered a solitary answer: go on up the mountain walls. The Mountaineer spoke. We went on up.

We were about 200 feet above the loch bound for 'a good campsite in the corrie' when the wind arrived. As far as I could tell, it hit us vertically from above, a single, stunning hammer-blow gust. A second gust blew wet, something undefinable, like snow but it was *June* and it didn't snow in June. The third 'gust' lasted ten minutes and drove us under cover amid some boulders. In those ten minutes our sheltering rock of pink granite furred white. Yep, snow. I looked down towards the loch in time to see the snow cloud slide a gray shutter across the last few yards of water at its southern end (the same sandy beach where an hour ago I had contemplated a swim), then the loch was gone. Still the wind bore down, flattening shafts of demented, freezing air. There now seemed little to choose between corrie and loch. Urged on by the Mountaineer's assurance that the one 'was only 1000 feet higher' than the other, we climbed, pushing our bowed heads ever deeper into a hanging, barging porridge of airy snow.

Coire Dhondail scared me rigid, or rather, what I could see of it did. It was not a source of comfort that the two tents would have to be pitched in the same pile-driver winds, nor that I was to share with the Bluffer. He reminded me then of a weekend golfer whose clubs and clothing were the envy of all the clubhouse and who knew how to use none of it. The Bluffer had a new tent, stove, two jackets, ice-axe, gaiters, boots, pack, and much else besides. All that his equipment lacked was know-how. The tent was a curious species, like the top of a covered wagon with an igloo entrance grafted on to one end. The theory was that you put the back end of the thing into the wind, thus sparing the long-hooped flanks from broadside assaults. It is not a theory devised for the practice of camping in a corrie at 3000 feet up Braeriach. In the corrie, the wind had stopped pile-driving. Instead, it had become a berserk merry-go-round. The Mountaineer's tent was up in minutes, low and dark and sure of itself. He came over, contemplating assistance, took one contemptuous look at the raw material he would be assisting (enough tent material to canopy a hot air balloon, enough two-legged balloons to suggest that in this wind it had a fair chance of flying), snorted, swore, and stalked off back to his tent from which salt-in-the-wound smells of soup and coffee had just reached us on one of the wind's circular frenzies.

It took an hour. The Bluffer explained that the tent had never been pitched before. The sight of him standing in that dark and primitive scoop on the flank of (for me) the mightiest mountain in the land, holding an instruction leaflet in one hand while the wind sought to prise the tent from our three remaining knuckle-white, finger-blue hands is with me still. I hope it haunts him. A particularly hell-bent wind arrived and I watched aghast as he let go of the tent to hold the paper taut in both hands. Then he realised what he had done, flailed after the tent, and the instruction leaflet was heading for the Moine Mhor, crossing Gleann Einich fast at 3000 feet and climbing.

It would be unlikely, he said, that it would ever be 'this tricky' again. 'Pitching the tent, I mean,' he said. The evening would prove him right. The next hour saw to it that the tent would never be pitched again.

We were installed. We were wet, insufferably cold, irritable, and we were being slapped in the face every few minutes by a sodden tent wall as the wind flayed on. But we were installed. The Bluffer was at the back of the tent and I was at the entrance, an arrangement I had insisted on. My insistence may well have saved both our lives. My stove was thawing out a pan of soup near the igloo aperture which by merciful chance I had declined to close, pleading claustrophobia. My back was to the Bluffer, my eyes wandering between the stove and the rough circle of mountain world at the end of the short igloo tunnel, my mind dwelling unhealthily on where this wretched tent was pitched, and what would happen if it failed to survive a night of such winds. Then the Bluffer's voice: 'Oh shit! I've dropped it!'

There is a short list of two rules concerning the changing of gas cyclinders on small camping stoves. It goes like this:

(1) Not in an enclosed space.

(2) Not near a naked flame.

The tent was enclosed space defined, my lit stove was the naked flame, and that thing rolling across the tent floor and coming to rest against my leg was a gas cylinder, spilling gas. I picked it up and threw it down the igloo tunnel: it had travelled perhaps eighteen inches from my hand when it exploded; it reached the outside world a flaming missile just as the Mountaineer emerged from his tent on a goodwill visit.

The next thing I remember clearly is rolling on a bank of old snow beating out the flames on my cagoule and the Mountaineer towering over me and shouting in a fury of incomprehension. 'What *the fuck* are you doing?'

Then I realised my face felt hot and the rest of me sick. His tone changed. 'Shit. Are you alright?'

I was shocked to discover that I was. Hair and eyebrows were singed, but otherwise I was undamaged. The same could not be said for the tent. The fireball had put two substantial holes in the floor and wall before the Bluffer had smothered the flames. He now emerged on all fours, and wearing an expression which I realised at once was the origin of the phrase 'a sheepish grin'. He said, 'Your soup's boiling.'

The second wind was a bully. I have written about it once before in my book, *A High and Lonely Place* (*The Sanctuary and Plight of the Cairngorms*), but the memory of it then was still raw and new, a weal on the mind. But in an epilogue to that book, I wrote that '. . . you cannot have the mountain blow you from its old rock reassurances like an autumn leaf and not learn something about the mountain and the leaf'. This second scrutiny of that wind is about what I have learned from it.

That expedition with the Bluffer and the rest helped to put me off mountaineering groups for life. Now I go mostly alone, occasionally with a kindred spirit. The day of the second wind I was alone on a buoyant spring-skied April day, climbing again out of Gleann Einich towards a different flank of Braeriach, intent on the mountain's still centre, Coire an Lochain. Many mountain miles and twenty years had passed since the day of the exploding tent, and, as I thought, every shape and shade of mountain wind.

The Cairngorms . . . 'tracts of winds as Arctic as the terrain can ambush you from behind the smokescreen of a breeze'

Gleann Einich in deceptive sunshine while storms war on the great plateau of the high Cairngorms

So the first thing I learned from that wind in particular was – in the Cairngorms of all places – to be perpetually vigilant for the deceptions of nature. There is a danger if you come through unscathed as many mountain years as I had from my first Sidlaw stumblings to the day of this second wind, that you pack a species of complacency with your compass and your camera and your lunch. Perhaps the day you decide, however subconsciously, that the hill has nothing left in its repertoire to surprise you with is the day you walk into such a wind as this.

The store of my Cairngorms years is rich, well lined with not just the rewards of hard endeavour but also great good fortune. It may be that I had come to set too much store by my luck, not enough in the *need* to go thoughtfully and warily and to see the deceptions of nature for what they are. There are usually signs to be read, but only by watching eyes, willing to read.

Gleann Einich that day was Eden, the waters of the Beanaidh Bheag an elixir, honeyed and tangy as sloe gin. I paused in my drinking to look out across the folds of that hugely furrowed mountain mass, a landscape fashioned by the ploughshares of glaciers, a climbing, blanketing heathery boulderfield which, by its very scale and crumpled grandeur, speaks to you of elemental and ancient forces. It tells you that here is a landscape too fixed and final for people, where the forces which still prevail are too primitive, too gargantuan; your place, it says, is down there, in the glen, the forest, the plain, the shore. It is watching these great clambering corrugations, depth on depth of them, rumpling the pelt and furrowing the brow of that single stupendous mountain we call 'the Cairngorms', which has advised me best about the nature of that landscape, its might, its scale, its Arctic-ness, its uniqueness.

Why there, on that ill-defined bank of an unsung burn?

Why not on the summits? The troughs of the great passes? The bitten and spewed bowls of the corries? The high roller-coastering miles of the plateaux which collide with unhindered skies?

I think it has to do with the sense of a ribcage, the bared torso of the mountain. If you look at one of those furrows, run your eye up and down its climbing mile until you lose it in the moor-wide plateau or the tapering glen, and hold that in your mind's eye as a single rib, or a single vertebra perhaps, you begin to grapple with the notion of the Cairngorms as a single mountain of immense proportions. Perhaps the grappling will help you to understand the worth of where you stand. Perhaps the grappling will leave your mind numb and unable to grasp anything, but in that case you will have learned something else, just as valuable, for the scale of the mountain will have been enough to confound your best efforts and that fact alone should help to convince you of the extraordinariness of the Cairngorms landscape. Most mountains you will encounter in Scotland are clearly distinguishable in shape and summit and sides. In the Cairngorms, the only mountain definition which makes any sense is the one that encompasses the whole landmass. When you stand on the bank of the Beanaidh Bheag and look north or north-east, you see the flanks of what the map defines as three mountains, Braeriach, Carn Elrig, and, beyond the hidden Lairig Ghru, Cairngorm. But they all flow so seamlessly into each other, stamped with the same Arctic hallmark that you cannot make a case for conserving one portion of the landmass without making a case for all of it, nor can you claim that it is safe to develop a small area of the greater landmass without tarnishing the whole.

All this was fermenting into a feverish brew in my mind when I walked headlong into the kind of wind which befits such an elemental realm. I felt it first as I climbed out of the burn's small gorge and immediately its impact troubled me. In the high boulderfield beneath Braeriach's trinity of north-facing corries it began to chill the air markedly. I know now with the benefit of hindsight and careful reconstruction of the day, that there was a point then when I appreciated that I was taking on more than I had any right to if I chose to climb on. This wind was trouble. In choosing to climb alone, I have never knowingly climbed beyond my limitations. I told myself that now. I told myself that the wind would only worsen as the day grew and I climbed higher. I told myself I was pushing my luck. Then I pushed it.

I suppose I was at about 2500 feet when the wind blew me over. I was boulder-hopping, a fast and effective method of traversing – or climbing – a boulderfield if you can achieve balance and rhythm and momentum. The wind saw to it that I achieved none of these. I stood and clambered on and it blew me over again. I weigh thirteen-and-a-bit stones, and mostly I am strong and fit: I was not to be taken lightly. I climbed on, and the wind flattened me again, and this time I hurt myself when I fell.

This time I sat still in the lee of a rock and ate a marshmallow, a morale booster. But the marshmallow was never invented which could offset the worst excesses of the Cairngorms, and I finally acknowledged a new component in the situation. Fear. I was afraid of the wind.

Fear can do two things to a solitary man on a mountain. It can invoke panic or it can induce a new respect for the mountain which translates into either the discretion of retreat or the valour of climbing with a quite exhilarating sense of awareness and care. Both courses are honourable, but in such circumstances as I now found myself, honour was worth less than a crushed crumb of pink gravel. Nine times out of ten I would have turned back, given that I was alone, but today was the tenth, and I was urged on by a mischievous and spirited sixth sense, and a sense of pilgrimage too, which had attended my climb from the first. For I was on the mountain, not to climb it, not to pee on the cairn and pronounce it conquered, but to trek up to its innermost sanctum, the highest loch in Scotland, Loch Coire an Lochain. I was in search of the mountain's secrets, my prime motive in being on any mountain anywhere, and it now seemed to me, my senses heightened by the extremes of the mountain's mood, that here was a supreme test of that declared motive. I brandished my fear of the wind, and in brandishing it, climbed through it.

The wind knocked me over so often that I began to move ready to roll with its punches. I would try to forestall the felling gusts by sitting down, beating them to the punch. I didn't succeed often, but often enough to make me *listen* to the wind, to unravel its meaning, to try and fathom its speech, to confront the confused language of one more of the mountain's secrets.

The gust which ushered me yards sideways and on to an old and frozen snowslope was a particularly misinterpreted piece of that secretive vocabulary, and by the time I had recovered from a more-or-less uncontrolled slide 200 feet back down Braeriach, my spirits were briefly dampened enough to prompt breathless reappraisal. I sat in the lee of one more boulder (coffee, chocolate, a consoling dram) and concluded that nothing had changed except that I had been clumsy and lucky. The wind – and the fall – had a message for me, however, which I now understood all too well. Stop. Rest. Take stock. I think I had been blown over thirteen times, and had taken more than two hours to climb a little less than 1000 feet, 200 of which I would now have to climb again. The slog had become the journey, instead of the means to achieve a good purpose. The rest restored the purpose. I let my thoughts linger on that pilgrim purpose.

Of all mountains, the Cairngorms are the ones I have always wanted to learn to know better, to understand more clearly, because of all my native landscapes, theirs is the one which truly merits the overworked accolade, unique. Their uniqueness is a bright lure in my mind always. Seton Gordon knew them, perhaps understood them better than any man, and in his 1924 book *The Cairngorm Hills of Scotland* he wrote of icebergs and waterspouts on Loch Coire on Lochain. I know of no one else who has seen such a thing in such a place and I had watched the day and listened to the weather

forecast and tried to translate the benevolence of the glen into the heightened realm of the high-mountain weather. Here, I decided, was an iceberg-and-waterspouts day. The wind was all that my mental image of such a phenomenon could ask for. Jigging and reeling waterspouts jousting with iceberg dodgems in a high and white-walled arena surely justified the day's endurance and endeavour. Surely the acquired secrets are more highly valued if they are well won.

I have cautioned many people many times against underestimating the Cairngorms, only because I have done it myself so often. I now did it again. I wrote about it thus in *A High and Lonely Place*:

> . . . at last the ground fell before me, and I was gingering down into the corrie itself, peering through stinging gustfuls of blown iced snow for the spectacle of the loch. There was none.
>
> I sat down again, dumbfounded this time. No loch?
>
> Not the wrong corrie?
>
> I reassured myself . . . three corries, and this the third one.
>
> A white wall climbed impenetrably upwards to where threshing clouds occasionally unveiled a black buttress and sank mysteriously downwards to a smooth and dazzling white corrie floor. This bowl of brilliant light was what had deceived. As the eyes accustomed to its glare I found a darker white stain and a network of awesome cracks, inches wide, feet deep. Then the sun began to spill out, first for moments then for minutes at a time, so that the light in the corrie flashed and coloured and blued and greyed and revolved as though it was playing off one of those 1950s ballroom globes. I was in the right corrie, and I had my spectacle, but it was not a thing of waterspouts and icebergs because the loch was under six feet of ice and frozen snow. The dark white stain showed where the snow had almost blown clear of the ice.

That corrie that day had all the icy smoothness of a marbled tomb, all the exaltation of a cathedral, all the tension of a coliseum. But these are comparisons which diminish its reality: I might have settled for them were it not for the arduous nature of the climb and the deceptions of wind and mountain to which I had succumbed. I reached the corrie with every nerve-end aglow, my sensitivity to my surroundings working with electric intensity. This was the inner sanctum of Braeriach, as I fancied it; I had thought of it as a still centre, an observation based on previous glimpses of it looking down from the plateau 1000 feet above; I had prepared myself today for a place giddy with spectacle, a fairground of nature; instead, it was a place of a stillness such as I had never known. Oh, the wind still flailed at the walls and corkscrewed up the headwall, but here it was a contained wind. That irresistible force which had so tormented me was tamed and redirected by the immoveable mountain.

And then, as I remembered those high-summer plateau days when I looked down

PREVIOUS PAGE: Coire an Lochain . . . 'all the icy smoothness of a marbled tomb, all the tension of a coliseum . . .'

on the loch, I pictured this gaunt and forbidding mountain arena as nothing more than a pocket in that Arctic garb which clothes the Cairngorms.

And then, I found the ptarmigan feather I described in Chapter Two, and I was seven years old and on my knees and all that had changed was the scope of my capacity to wonder.

The third wind was an absence. I think of a moment in the company of that absent wind as one of the most moving in my life. A moment is all there was of it, too, for in the moment was the recognition of the rarest and purest phenomenon in nature.

Silence.

To mark the silence was to break it, and the first uncanny moment was gone, but if your mind runs to contemplating such intangibles as a mountain heartbeat, the sound of that single ancient silence was surely its pulse.

I was in good company for such a vivid occurrence. No one has written with more profound eloquence about mountaineering than David Craig in his *Native Stones*, or about Highland people in his *On the Crofters' Trail*. The bond between man and the mountain landscape is both a psychological and creative force within him. On the day of the third wind, we were climbing together for the first time, and taking a risk. Twenty-four hours earlier we had met for the first time in a bar in Aviemore after the briefest of correspondence. But he had read a book of mine, and I had read one of his, and on the strength of the obvious common ground, he invited me to join him on a Cairngorms ploy. The risk was keeping the company of a total stranger for five days in a landscape beloved by both of us. But it worked, and we worked, and after a fruitless soaking in vile equinoctial weather, we stepped out from Glen Feshie to cross the Moine Mhor on a morning of autumnal prime.

The old name for the Cairngorms is Monadh Ruadh, Red Mountains; they might have been named for such a day. Their every shade varied that single red theme, the grasses and the finished heather, buttress and scree, shadow and shore and plateau. We were far out into the Moine Mhor, that high mountain sea which undulates between three and four thousand feet (yet still the great summits of Braeriach, Cairn Toul, Sgor an Lochain Uaine rise above it, unfurled breakers). Here is the Arctic heart of the Cairngorms, a land without limit under skies which seem to overlap it, like Orkney heaved up out of its ocean. It is, like Orkney, normally a place of flattening winds, but all day we had been walking among nothing more than breezes. We were suddenly aware in the same instant that our feet made the only sound in the landscape. The wind had gone, and its going stopped us dead. Incomprehension held us for a few seconds, then we heard it: nothing. No sound. No shred of wind, no whisper of it round a rock or through a tuft, no small tug at an ear. Nothing. No fall of water, neither trickle on rock nor slap on shore. No cataract, no single syllable of water. Nothing. No bird call. No deer gutturals, no bleat of sheep, no footfall, no voice, no far vehicle, no dog bark, no aircraft drone. We were too far out on to the Moss to hear anything other than the Moss's own sounds, and for these few seconds it offered none at all.

Coire an Lochain, grandest of Braeriach's trinity of north-facing corries

The Moine Mhor . . . 'that high mountain sea . . . the Arctic heart of the Cairngorms . . . a land without limit . . .'

We were still, pillars of stone. I said:

'Listen.' I regret the word now, for it besmirched the silence, but it had the effect of listening harder, and the harder we listened, the more vast the silence, the more acute that wondrous symbolic nothing, a mountain heartbeat, or a glimpse of nature asleep.

Then, the faintest sound I ever remember, a flake of a thing, audible only because of the silence it greeted, the flight speech of wild geese reached us. My first response was to question whether I heard the thing at all, but there it was again from high, high, so high. We scanned the sky, but again the Cairngorms' way with unfathomable scale defeated us. How high do you look when you are at 3500 feet, and a skein of geese of all raucous things reaches you from above, soft as a sliver of a sigh? We found them at last, crossing the mountains fully 2000 feet up, quite possibly much higher, but moving steadily south at between 5000 and 7000 feet.

We have between us sixty or more years of wandering wild places. We could remember no such silence. Perhaps it occurs in mid-Sahara, or the Australian outback. Mostly, when it occurs at all, it will be the preserve of the Arctic.

The geese trembled beyond our earshot, the breeze was restored, and our footfalls resumed. But in my head, from that day to this, I can still remember the sense, if not the sound, of soundlessness, the breathlessness of the third wind.

Chapter Four

THE BEAUTIFUL FRIENDSHIP

BEN LEDI IS a frontier mountain. The road north-west out of Stirling cat-and-mouses with its sprawled and imperfect pyramid. Each new sighting advances the mountain, redefining its lynch-pin role in Scotland's Southern Highland skyline. Stirling, they like to say down the road a bit, is the buckle at Scotland's waist which clasps Highland and Lowland together, in which case Ben Ledi is a dark jewel in Scotland's navel. The flat lands of the Carse to the west of Stirling do not prepare you for the speed of the mountain's advance, but when you emerge from the woods beyond Doune, it has begun to dominate all it surveys and the eyes of all who survey it. By the time you have submitted to the tourism-tattooed maw of Callander the mountain has become an impassable wall. It is not impassable, of course, but only because centuries ago travellers took their courage in their hands and dared a tortuous way through the Pass of Leny, first and last portal of the Highlands, depending on the way your prejudices lie. Either way, the landscape beyond it is changed irrevocably, and whether it welcomes or ousts you to or from the Highlands, Ben Ledi is a fitting ambassador to what lies beyond or behind.

But unwise counsel has prevailed hereabouts in recent years, and my disaffection for what Ben Ledi had become prompted the following article in the magazine *Climber and Hillwalker* in 1989:

THE BEAUTIFUL FRIENDSHIP has ended after twenty years. I think I will not go back to Ben Ledi.

In all that time, it has been a significant mountain dignifying my skyline, a handsome, satisfying reassurance of mountain lands beyond. It is in that guise, too – a Highland harbinger – that legions of visitors encounter Ben Ledi every year as they trek north-west out of Callander into the tightening throat of the Pass of Leny. It is a watershed of landscapes, a portal of a mountain kingdom.

The truth is that the friendship has grown progressively less beautiful with the years to the point at which almost every dignifying mountain feature has been defiled. It happened this way:

43

Time was when there were two ways to climb Ben Ledi. Either you slogged up a string of undeviating merciless false summits from Loch Venacharside, or you threaded the Forestry Commission's vague track up through the Stank Glen, the dark side of the mountain overlooking the Pass of Leny. There were other ways, of course, but they diverted you mightily, along paths and over hills where mostly you had no wish to be diverted.

Then, in the mid-1970s, the Commission had an acute fit of public accountability compounded by all the symptoms of the new and fashionable 'countryside facilities' disease, and a cancerous species of rot set in. Worse, it was deliberately implanted. A signposted path was hacked up the mountainside through the forest to a stile on a deer fence, and cairned and waymarked across the face of the hill to join the old yak route up from Loch Venachar high on the south shoulder. A car park was built at the bottom of the path. Then the car park was too small. Then the car park was enlarged.

The mountain relented. The forest path wilted to a morass. The deer fence stile became quite unreachable because it had been sited on the surface of a peat bog. Now that brutal weekend regiments of waymarked feet had removed the surface of the bog, the stile rose ingloriously from a small sea of chocolate milkshake. Higher up, or higher down, the regiments had simply flattened the fence, the way regiments on the march do. They slavishly followed the waymarkers and the cairns and obeyed the signposts, the way regiments on the march do. Small bands of guerillas burying waymarkers and demolishing cairns could not mitigate the effects of such overwhelming odds.

A few of us voiced our fears in print again and again over the years. We were branded as 'elitist', a thoughtless taunt based on the false premise that we sought to save the mountains for ourselves. Rubbishing the critics became the countryside establishment's way of avoiding the issue. Protest about the rights of landscape for its own sake, the desecration of the sanctity of mountains, were dismissed – at best as outrageous exaggeration, at worst as the ravings of a lunatic fringe.

Well, on Ben Ledi the mountain landscape's rights have now been trampled underfoot, its sanctity swamped. Sustained vandalism of the landscape has been practised and presided over here to match all the worst urban excesses which our society is so quick to condemn, yet it has progressed with the official encouragement of a government body. The mountain is in rags.

It was perhaps two years since I had last climbed Ben Ledi, my own visits becoming less frequent as the beauty of the friendship diminished and the enlarged car park overflowed. But on a cool, still April evening I climbed again. I aimed to be on the summit by seven and walk down the Stank in the dusk, hoping against hope to cement bonds anew, knowing that in the intervening years the Commission had made a token gesture towards persistent public criticism and removed waymarkers from the open hill.

I found not a forest path but a linear building-site. The new path, which is being painstakingly laid on the morass of the old, confers on the mountain forest all the

'There is a place among the fields to the south of the mountain where I stop to watch it . . .'

subtlety of a garden centre. I cannot deny that it is preferable to the morass but that is all I cannot deny. It is a thankless and futile task the path-makers pursue here, for the regiments, the feet, the frosts, the snows, the rains, the winds, will all unhinge their best efforts, and without a commitment by the Commission to constant maintenance of the path for all time, they always will.

The problem begets other problems. The car park and the marked trail fall prey to the eager talons of the tourist industry, an unexacting host in much of the Highlands, and are publicised accordingly. A species of non-mountaineer becomes acquainted with the fact that Ben Ledi is a belittled mountain, paved and waymarked and tamed, a kind of vertical public path. He is not a seeker after mountain solaces but a herdsman. He manipulates mass events, hill races, sponsored this-and-thats, mini-buses full of outdoor education. The tourism budget is big enough for all of them. The car park isn't quite but it can always be enlarged. Only the mountain itself cannot handle them.

But the mountain has become the last consideration as the mood of permissive destruction becomes all-pervasive. I began angrily to demolish a cairn high on the mountainside, only to discover that it had been constructed to conceal fourteen empty beer cans, a small monument to the rubbishing of a mountain.

From here too, I saw what looked like a tall crucifix among the summit rocks. I was already vexed by the outrages of the lower mountain and the cairn. I found only anger at the new intrusion. It proved to be exactly what it seemed, a tall iron crucifix with a small metal plaque screwed into the rock at its base, a memorial to a mountain rescue team member who had died (on a different mountain) and whose friends and kin saw in the gesture a fitting tribute.

I wonder. I, like anyone who has a lifetime in the mountains for a heritage, can understand the grief of the mountain-bereaved. We, the lucky ones, all know someone who didn't come back or came back maimed, or someone who was particularly cruelly treated – an acquaintance in Edinburgh, for example, who lost both her brother and her father to the Scottish mountains. My antipathy towards permanent memorials in the mountains stems not so much from the fact that if everyone who so died was so commemorated the mountains would be forests of crosses, although that should perhaps be a consideration. It is rather that in the case of every mountaineer I can think of who puts an inestimable value on the mountain itself, they will hold that the wild mountain is memorial enough.

The problem with a mountain like Ben Ledi, or at least what Ben Ledi has become, is that it is an unconvincing argument which pleads for the mountain ethic when the mountain ethic has been so blatantly and ruthlessly diluted over the years. It becomes easier to plant a cross – a cross of all things – if it is already accepted in the public perception of Ben Ledi that it is a mountain with which liberties can be taken. But why not plant a birch, an oak, a rowan?

I circled the mountain's eastern corrie, dropped down into the Stank, there to be greeted by a sign informing uphill walkers, 'Waymarking ends here', as though it were a hazard to be contemplated like 'Beware of the Bull'. Then I found that the Commission had employed a new species of waymarking for the glen – painted wooden footprints (green for uphill, yellow for down), and that even this least-frequented corner of the mountain was in the throes of being smashed into a pulpy oblivion because people have been directed there where once they had to find their own way and mostly didn't bother.

So it is a weary burden I bear down from the mountain, because I sense that Ben Ledi's brave skyline poise is an illusion. It is a defeated mountain. Worse, it is not the only one. The Commission has wrought similar fates on Ben Venue and Ben A'an in the Trossachs, products of the same misguided philosophy. I take it badly with Ben Ledi because I know it best, because it has suffered most, because it is such a symbolic mountain.

It could be redeemed by closing the car park, removing the waymarkers, 'resting' the beleaguered ground and according the landscape its due. But the longer the situation persists the less likely is a cure, because the 'facilities' are now cogs in the tourist publicity machine too, and that is a weightier juggernaut than even the Forestry Commission, and tougher to brake or deflect from its set course.

Scotland has lost sight of the fundamental truth which guided our trail-blazing landscape heroes – John Muir, Seton Gordon, Frank Fraser Darling, Percy Unna, W.H. Murray. The landscape itself, for its own sake, was the first of all their priorities. Ben Ledi, the Hill of Light, is now only a symbol of the darkness with which we have cloaked their vision.

The magazine sub-editor's headline for the article had been DEATH OF A MOUNTAIN. Months after it appeared, I stumbled on it again when I was looking for something else. I re-read it with all the old anger intact, but then, after I had considered the headline, I was caught unawares by another emotion. Guilt. Was the mountain really dead? Unquestionably it was in the poorest health of its life, but if I was claiming a beautiful friendship with a mountain (a phrase which first sounded a shade pretentious but then the more I thought about it rang truer and truer), by what code of ethics could I justify turning my back on it? I concede that to many people such an idea may jar uncomfortably, yet I believed then (I believe it now more than ever) that I owed the mountain a debt for all it had unlocked for me over more than twenty years. The debt could not be repaid by absence, any more than it could be simply by continuing to climb the mountain and growing angry in the process. The anger had served its purpose, drawing the mountain's plight to the attention of thousands of climbers through the article, prompting a considered response in many letter-writers. But if I could study the mountain? If I could try to fathom a better understanding of it, and through that singular mountain, understand all mountains better? *There* was a way to begin to repay Ben Ledi.

Besides, I am more susceptible to the lure of such a mountain than most people, and my travels compel me to watch it or consider it or drive among its shadows so often

that I rescinded my pledge to stay away and set about rebuilding my love of the place. There is, for example, a place among the high fields to the south of the mountain where I stop to watch it. It is a good place to watch because it sets the mountain in its landscape context, lording it over the farms and woods and foothills and setting a small village spire against it. The viewpoint emphasises how such a mountain must once have dominated human lives. It is no coincidence that among the unconvincing theories about Ben Ledi's name are two which venture 'Mountain of God' and 'Mountain of Light'. (These are much the same thing: all we can ask of our Gods is that they shed a little light on our lives.) If there is any substance to them at all – and who knows? – it hints at a regard for the mountain which may well have been sacred at some time, and there is no denying its impressive stance over the lives of the farm folk who toil within its aura.

So at every opportunity, I began to stop and watch the mountain, watch its response to light and season and day and dusk and night, snow and moon, storm and calm, and soon the idea that 'Ben Ledi's skyline poise is an illusion' was beginning to crumble. When you watch a mountain this closely, it looms larger in your life than its mere physical mass. It acquires stature and puts a sensible perspective on human endeavour. My approach to the mountain grew more thoughtful, so that if I drove out to climb it or simply to keep its company in some way, I would stop two or three times on the way, relishing the mountain's advance, its slow re-shaping, its emerging detail. Then, when I immersed myself in its shadow, burrowing a privately worked alley up through its forest, I would have in my mind my images of Ben Ledi as a distant mountain, and the size and shape and scope of the mountain I climbed. Most mountains do not offer that opportunity, but rummaging through my own preferences, I find several which do, and I love them the more for it. Ben Ledi's speciality is that it stands proud from the mountainous land beyond and contemplates the mountainless land to the south so that you approach it from other realms where mountains do not hold sway and suddenly realise that in all the horizons at your disposal, your eye is fastened compulsively to its profile.

I sit under a broken rock the size of a house (I like to reverse the simile – my house is the size of the broken boulder on Ben Ledi) shutting out a blizzard from my mind, and thinking instead of how the mountain would look right now as it whitens distantly from the good place among the high fields to the south. Perhaps only the bottom half of the mountain will be visible beneath the storm's seething. Perhaps the wind will be blowing rags of cloud across the higher slopes so that it drops snowy hints of the torment its whip-hand inflicts on the higher slopes. I have been here a quiet hour now, having seen the storm advance from the summit ridges and having retreated down a favoured leeward face under a high corrie. Here the slopes are host to a teeming congregation of rocks – blunt and broad, slender and spired, spikey, hunched, loners

PREVIOUS PAGE: Ben Ledi is a frontier mountain, a fitting ambassador to Highland landscapes beyond

and crowds, but all contained within the single mountain face so that it looks as if they have been planted there, a seedbed of would-be mountains. On the one hand, it would be good to transplant a few, to thin them a bit, and make new mountains in the sad landscapes which have none. On the other, this crowded mountainside is a majestic tumbledown. Once, the earth opened here and spat chunks of mountain far into the air: they fell where Ben Ledi, as yet infantile and unformed, had prepared a sticky seedbed for them. They adhered as they landed, and there they still adhere, some pretending to be mountains, some exchanging ice-age truths, debating eternity's laws.

Sorley MacLean, matchless poet of Gaeldom, saw something similar (allowing for differences of scale) in what I have long held to be his best poem, 'Kinloch Ainort': the relevant Gaelic line is:

còrr-lios bheanntan fàsmhor

which he translates as:

a great garth of growing mountains

The head of Loch Ainort on Skye butts into a flank of the Red Cuillin. You stand at sea level and stare up at an encircling glower, a dark arc of peaks. 'Garth' is an enclosed garden, and 'còrr-lios' translates, however crudely, as a peaked garden. It is a good garth of growing mountains, if not a great Cuillin-esque one, which throngs the face of Ben Ledi in the eyes of one boulder-crouching, blizzard-cowering mortal. I have clambered over this mountainside many times in every weather and season, but this one clambering stands out from all the others, because of the fox.

I have come on the shelter of the boulder from above, fumbling in next to no visibility, meeting the storm head-on in my last few downhill yards. Windshriek and snow-veil have obliterated sight and sound and scent of me. The lee of my rock is gratefully and breathlessly achieved. I know my way on down, but not blindfold. I will give the weather a chance to exhaust itself. There are too many pitfalls and untrustworthy footings between here and the forest path: holes among rocks, cracks among slabs, small cliffs trembling under unsteady boulders, all coated in new wet snow. Three hours of daylight left, a good torch in the pack, no reason to hurry, let the mountain have its say and listen. So I sit an hour and watch and listen to the mountain as it whitens. The coffee steams, a small whisky burns cheerfully. It is a good place to be, quiet and alone, familiar yet invigorated by the spine-stiffening storm and the perpetual expectancy of the unexpected. I tell myself again . . . a good place to be quiet and alone, and (the way it happens sometimes so that you suspect some trivial conspiracy of nature and mountain) in the same instant I know that I am not alone. A

The boulder, birthmark on the face of the mountain, shelter for stormbound climber and fox

A favourite perch on Ben Ledi's summit ridge contemplates a wide swathe of the Southern Highlands

rough heathery slope, perhaps ten feet from top to bottom and a yard wide, slithers away from the boulder which protects my overhanging shelter from the east. The wind is a barging south-westerly, so all the boulder achieves today is to encumber a wide view of the mountainside. But it has also hidden a fox from me (and me from the fox) for perhaps as much as an hour. I reach for the rucksack to pour a second cup of coffee and crane a weather eye out over the boulder. There is a small couch at the foot of the heather slope. On the couch, coiled as a watchspring, lies a sleeping red fox, turning white. The couch is a shelf on the edge of a buttress where a wide groove in the rock channels a fluke of the snow-wind and contrives to lather the fox's curved spine with a thin but perceptibly thickening wedge of snow. But for that chance eddying of the wind, the fox has chosen superbly, the comfort of the heathery couch, the storm-shelter, and the wide mountain view which my harder, drier bolt-hole is denied.

The moments consolidate. I have not dared to breathe in what seems an unduly long eternity, probably half a minute. Every limb has stiffened. I can hear a hammerbeat, my inconsiderate heart. Surely the fox is not deaf to that racket! Surely he is not impervious to the rhythmic tremor down through the rock! Relax. Breathe out, for God's sake. Think about this. He hasn't heard you clattering about for the flask and the pack. In that wind, how could he?

He doesn't know you're here!

I withdraw, begin to work silently, lay spare jacket and pack behind the boulder and lie on them so that I can peer over the rock in what passes for comfort in such a place. I watch, unwatched. His flank moves, steadily, lightly. Snow touches it and melts, touches, melts. The face of him is hidden. The snow wedge round his spine is two inches tall now, and as wide at the bottom, tapering to nothing as it climbs his back.

Ten minutes. The snow gains another half inch. I grow as numb as my sheltering rock. He ceases to be fox in my mind but a small abstraction of the mountain, a cushion of colour with its own foothills, shoulders, summits, the shades of autumn transplanted into the mountain's midwinter. Put him in autumn bracken and you could walk past him at five paces, unsuspecting.

Fifteen minutes. Only the flank has moved. Perhaps an eye is alert. I cannot tell. The snow is thinning, and makes no further progress up his back. Then, just like that, he stands. A ripple goes through him and the snow avalanches down from his spine. He is at once tall, poised, noticing, testing, thinking, fox. But the weather is with me and he can't catch my drift. Instead, he turns and begins to walk up the ramp *towards* me. The heart-hammer resumes. Be still! No sound, no betraying hint, not now. *Now* don't breathe!

Six feet away and in the darkest lee of the ramp he stops, lifts a foot like a pointer, leans at the wind, working it. What he sees of me is probably meaningless: eye slits far back in my hood, only that, the blackness of the inside of the rock behind me. But now he scents. He makes a fast left turn where I would have sworn there was no left to turn to, only an unyielding rock wall. And I hear his feet on my roof.

It takes perhaps twenty seconds to move to where I can see him go. He moves over the whitened mountain like a beacon, an easy lope carrying him round to where he can put the wind on me. He stands and stares back over his shoulder, but I don't put the glasses on him. I watch him as he watches me, and in the perspective and the scale of the mountain and the storm we are just a meeting of mites on the surface of permanence. I have come on the tracks of a mountain fox in countless snows. Now for the first time, I watch the birth of a mountain fox track, see one foot go in to the knee, see a soft puff of snow breath as he takes a slabby rock in his path with a single spring, four-footed on its crown, then down the other side, the loping trot resumed. The shortest distance between two foxes is a straight line. His line is through a morass of huge rocks, and there I lose him. He is gone, and the mountain is a good place to be quiet and alone again.

In the pub:
  'Been on the Hill again the day?'
  'Just the Ben.'
  'Wouldnae see much in that, eh?'
  'Not much. A big dog fox.'
  'Fox! Bastards. Just as soon shoot yin as look at it. Same again?'
  But I had gone, vanished like a fox among boulders.

For more than twenty years I have lived near enough to Ben Ledi to climb it in a summer evening. Four hours on the mountain are usually enough – up through the pungent trees, loud with roe-bark, cool and midgey (a tantalisingly frustrating combination after the heat of the day); up the mountain shoulder; a short cut up a tremulous gully eyeballing small goldenrod; across the summit with half an hour to linger high among favourite sunset rocks watching the west and the north where all my inclinations lie; leisurely round the corrie rim; down through the bouldery place of the fox; elatedly back through the dark green forest where the roe deer bark on, a loud asthmatic note unworthy of their summer graces. Anyone I met would be coming down as I climbed. Occasionally there is an offering of advice in passing, cautioning against the lateness of my ascent.

The evening mountain is an ordered layer cake of wildlife regimes. The roe deer, emboldened by the withdrawal of daytime man, go confidently through clearings and feed leisurely in the rides or far out on the open hill. The doe is heavily pregnant. A week or two from now you may see her dash out suddenly and supremely sure-footed over the bracken-and-rock-strewn treacheries of a steep clearing and stand in the darkening edge to put the wind on you and watch. At your feet you may find her preposterously pretty fawn, curved and quiet and still, and in the seductions of that early June evening and the all-encompassing mountain world and its light, you might look at the creature in the bracken and know why poets so love the word 'dappled'. Also: if you want that fawn to live wild and free and greet your mountain evenings of future seasons, leave it alone, not so much as a fingertip touch, for your scent on it is the one thing on the mountain its mother will not tolerate.

The treetops are the fiery preserve of red squirrels and jays, flashy extroverts both, and loud when they have a mind, which in the case of the jay is much of the time. In Gaelic, the jay is *sgreuchan coille*, 'screamer of the woods', and certainly nothing in all the woods of Gaeldom advertises its presence quite so recklessly, not since the last wolf's throat was cut. The red squirrel is the one nature gave us, as opposed to the gray, which is the one we had imposed on us by forces other than nature. In a forest like this, however, the red holds his own, admirably.

He stands on the sunset spire of a larch, and a wild fire blazes a halo about the summer sheen of him. He leans his head flat so that one ear faces the sky, suddenly warned and wary. I have heard it too, the conversation-stopper of the next layer of the mountainside. Buzzards preside between the treetops and the next 1000 feet of airspace, adrift on spirals and threnody. I see her briefly, leaning in against the rockface, head-down huntress. What rock climbers buzzards are, scaling a fifty-foot buttress without touching the rock. Not even Messner can do that.

The squirrel dives down, takes the first twenty vertical feet of trunk flat out, but his retreat from the buzzard has put him on a collision course with what is, from a squirrel's point of view, a greater threat. Me. He freezes twenty feet above the ground, head facing down the trunk, tail flattened and pointing up, four feet splayed wide and clinging. He looks like a hunter's trophy, a small hearth-rug skinned and spread wide, but he galvanises again, reverses his position in a single movement too fast for my eye to explain, sprints two vertical yards (Messner can't do that either), then hurtles through the twiggy spaces on to the next tree but one which he hits running. I climb on beyond the trees, smiling and shaking my head in bewildered admiration, to look for the buzzard.

She is not hard to find, for as she side-slips out across the forest she calls continually, a far-carrying down-curve of woodwind sound. She begins a new spiral, far enough out from the mountain shadow now to catch the sun, but only just far enough out, so that as she spirals she flies back into the unseen edge of shadow, then back into the light, shadow, light and constantly transforming herself vivid and dull, vivid and dull, and utterly oblivious to the mesmerism she works on watching eyes far below.

The south shoulder of the mountain on such an evening is a memorably yellow place. You have climbed into the uppermost layer of the mountain, the one which aborbs you beyond the ambiguities of the frontier and immerses you in the Highlands. A kestrel works the ridge, which is high for a kestrel, but on such an evening, the thermals buoy him up effortlessly, and nothing works the wind to more telling effect. The mountain is aglow in the lowering sun, the yellowness so fresh it looks as if it should come off on your boots. The mountains which peel away north and west to impossible distances (Mull? Jura?) are the world you have just entered, stacked and wedged tightly and grayly against each other, a crammed landscape. But you stand on the only yellow mountain in the land, and for a still summer hour you are in sole possession of its highest slopes.

I'm not much of a summit lingerer, for summits are where people gather, and to me there are few things less appropriate to a mountain summit than a gathering of people. Ben Ledi's evening summit is empty, but what with the commemorative cross and the souvenirs the day's summit lingerers had left behind (assorted cans, a plastic Irn Bru bottle, cigarette stubs, a Mars bar wrapper) I cross it without pause and rim the high hidden corrie where a favourite perch beneath the path stares out the sunset. On many a Scottish mountain this topmost layer is summer-shaved by red deer herds and overlorded by eagles, but Ben Ledi's steep flanks, girdling forest and out-on-a-limb stance probably discourage the deer, and eagles will almost always keep discreet distance between them and such a man-tormented mountain, such proximity to the Highland edge. Once in a while a young bird clasps an iced rock here in its first winter, but none lingers.

I have been warm and still and mildly intoxicated by the mountain brew for half an hour when a small and dowdy brown bird the size of a song thrush materialises on the heather six feet away, its presence announced by nothing more than a flutter of inarticulate wings. It is obviously newly fledged, but a newly fledged what? And why with an empty mountain at its stumbling disposal should it choose here, with my singularly unnatural blot on its landscape for company? And where is the adult whatever-it-is which should be keeping it company and teaching it not to seek out unnatural blots? The answers cross my bows at zero feet, flying in from the south while I faced west. The young bird had perched, it now transpires, with surprising judgment for one so young, for it has chosen a shallow dip on the crown of a small mound, a mound with the densest crop of blaeberries I have ever seen. What it has apparently not yet learned to do is pick them. But the flutter which caught my eye has also caught the eye of a parent bird seemingly as unconcerned by my presence as its offspring. The harsh pipe of its approach tells me all I need to know, and for that matter, what I should have guessed already.

There are few more brazen adventurers on the open hill than ring ousels. For the next ten minutes I watch with my best stillness while the adult crams its chick and itself with dozens and dozens of berries. The heart of its white breast crescent is a purple stain. I wonder idly how many times a high-summer ring ousel has been mis-diagnosed by birdwatching maniacs as an unidentifiable rarity on account of blaeberry juice.

The sun touches the north-west mountains and falls behind them, but there will be light in the sky for hours yet, and light of a kind in the north all night. There are many forms of contentment in the compass of human emotion: I know none more profound than to sit high and warm and still and watch the Highland landscape bare its soul to the forces of night.

(I see myself write the word 'soul'. The editor in my head sounds a cautionary note. 'You can't use that kind of stuff today. That's Wordsworth, eighteenth century.' I look at the word and I let it stand and I tell the voice in my ear: 'Good.')

An hour later, I am still sitting, still watching, mind cleansed by the healing airs and graces of the mountain I know best. Ahead of me is a long walk down through the shadows and the darkening forest, skirting the boulderfield where a ragged garden of alpine flowers scents the still air and hugs the rock for dear life. I was wrong. The beautiful friendship is not over. The mountain is not dead.

Chapter Five

AN IDEA CALLED HOME

THE BEALLACH AN DUBH CHOREIN joins the Siamese-twin mountains of Ben Vorlich and Stuc a' Chroin at the hip. It is a classic mountain crossroads. Two glens crampon up through corries to meet on the broad morass of rock and bog and hag; two mountain ridges, each miles long, dip to meet the two climbing glens. The bealach is where all their winds and all their stories commingle. Two mountain summits stand, abrupt as gateposts above it, so that nature seems to have thrust the centrepiece of the landscape not on the summits but on the pivotal hub of the bealach which locks them in their perpetual embrace.

The two glens might be one without that hump of granite and peat for a heaped bulwark. The two ridges might be one but for the ice-age yawn which the bealach holds in check like a good jawbone. Yet the two mountains so dominate the ends of their ridges, so stamp their character on that Southern Highland skyline that they would have been compelling individualists were it not for the bealach 1200 feet below which insinuates the two into one – 'Vorlich 'n' Stuc', practically one word.

Something central to my personal mountain philosophy is at work here, something about their very nature, and the way we perceive them: it is the summit shapes which define them from afar, but the closer you go, the deeper you penetrate among mountains, the more the summits recede, the more the mountain architecture reveals itself and compels. Consider a great building as thrown open to the sky as a mountain, a ruin like Holyrood Abbey in Edinburgh. You see it first as a gaunt and holed shape, decrepit perhaps but still shapely. But its glories are within; look up and see how its anonymous stone-masons simply curved the top of the walls inward and so formed the roof, one straight-faced stone on another, but forming a rising curve with no visible means of support. Ben Nevis is a blunt and bulky landmark from mountains 100 miles away, but stand under its north face and its ice-age stone masonry is one of the most astounding pieces of rock in our land. The Cuillin's gabbro hieroglyphics scribble their Skye-line across the vistas of a thousand viewpoints, but Coruisk is the gleaming kernel within the cracked and showy shell. Braeriach's architectural genius does not lie in the mighty plateau slab of its flat roof but in the vaulted chambers of its ring of

corries. And the Bealach an Dubh Chorein is Hercules slung between two mountainous pillars. The more you watch the bealach, the more you marvel at the miraculous bonding strength of the thing, holding landscapes together.

All this falls into its perspective as I plough a lonely north-eastering furrow from Callander towards the moorland pedestal of Uamh Bheag. As I walk, the two mountains slowly arrange and rearrange themselves. (Nature's scene-shifting can also be an end in itself among mountains rather than the force march to the summit. There is a fast way to the bealach and this is not it.) As I emerge from the forest, Stuc a' Chroin and Ben Vorlich emerge from a prime autumn morning's mist, folded behind the long south-westering shoulders of Gleann a' Chroin. What unfolds at first glance is a back-of-the-hand familiarity of mountain shapes and moorland undulations. Behind my glance is more than twenty years' worth of climbing and moor-wandering here, twenty years of watching the mountains work the same realignment trick, and still I do not tire of it. I pick out a point in the far foreground, half a mile ahead and to the left of my path, a rock with a broad pitched top and a kestrel pellet wedged into a fat vein of quartz. I cannot see the pellet or the quartz from this distance of course, but I know they are there from earlier seasons, the quartz cold however summer-warm the rock's touch might grow, the pellet as hardened and whitened as the small vole skull and skeleton it entombs. I measure my progress by the distance the rock appears to travel backwards against the mountain skyline. Soon the rock itself is behind me and I have moved a shoulder of the mountain so that it no longer veils the summit but leads my eye directly to the summit ridge. But that is only the first shoulder.

Stuc a' Chroin is disrobed, but Ben Vorlich and the Bealach an Dubh Chorein stand indiscreetly veiled behind the second shoulder. I cast ahead among the moor's low contours and my eye fastens on to a green mound still unbrushed by autumn's fiery reworking of the moor's colours. I tread my north-eastering groove again, reeling in the mound this time, measuring its progress towards Ben Vorlich, stalking a landscape.

Stealth creeps into my stride, not slowing it but making it more aware, more considered, more respectful of the landscape, more aware of all its gestures by homing in on one of them the way you can hear all the layers of an orchestra by homing in on the basses. With the stealth comes clarity, for I have begun to look harder at the landscape, and the more I watch a landscape, the more *it* reels *me* in. Nan Shepherd, Cairngorms poet and novelist, wrote, 'The thing to be known grows with the knowing' and it was never truer than in this familiar mountain landscape. The green mound is no longer a pawn in the mountains' scene-shifting game, but an island the moor sea cannot overwhelm, and like all islands it has its own shape, colours, contours, and its own life.

Can you go among mountains lifting your eyes not just to the summits and the

PREVIOUS PAGE: Stuc a' Chroin (left) and Ben Vorlich 'robed in the blaze shades of prime autumn . . .'

glittering ridges and the flightpaths of eagles, but also to the molehills of the mountain land, the rises on the moor and the foothills and all their fellow-travellers? There is no less mountain-ness among the footnotes of the landscape just because they spend much of their winter below the snow line. They remain in the mountains' thrall, no less a part of the experience of being among mountains whether your day's destination is a summit or a high pass or a moorland dawdle with the mountains purposely held at arms' length.

The green mound is host to a small dark silhouette which moves with small jerks and punctuates the jerks with small stillnesses. The appearance of a second silhouette a yard behind the first demands a closer scrutiny. The glasses snap the heads of two black grouse into focus. Now my stride's stealth comes into its own, earmarks the bed of a slow burn which gives a cautious approach to the mound. At twenty yards with the burn concealing my presence and muffling sound, there are not two black grouse but twelve. This is good news, for this pugilist of the wilds is a dwindling presence in Scotland, doomed it seems, by the relentless dwindling of its preferred habitat – pinewoods and moors like this one. For years I would find them here, then for years they were few or absent, shot and discouraged by sportsmen and bad winters to the verge of one more local extinction. Now they prosper again on this moor at least, and I crawl as close to the mound as the burn's low gully will allow, to refresh old memories.

Even now in early autumn, long after the mating season's passion is spent, a blackcock lek is a vigorous place in the first and the last of the light. Only in winter do the male birds tire of squaring up to each other, doubtless conserving energies for the harder bouts of survival. At every other season a mound like this one, or a woodland clearing, is a gladiatorial arena of some spectacle, but only in these private hours of low light. The birds gather to fight. Blows are aimed and struck with feet and beak, occasionally with a clubbing wing like a swan. Between blows there is much huffing and puffing, and in a bird the size of an overblown red grouse with vivid dark blue body, brown wings, blue lyre-shaped tail which falls away to display an erected dome of white tail feathers, even huffing and puffing is a convincing intimidation. As daylight waxes, the birds' energies wane, and the protagonists feed companionably enough until dusk when the madness revives. It is a baffling society which thirls itself to a green mound under the mountains.

It is noon on the mound. The birds are quiet. But as I turn to leave, an ill-considered boot dislodges a stone, and its clatter on to a small rock puts the birds to flight. They fly east, then north, then put a long curve towards the west across the moor. As they fly with the wind strumming their lyre tails, they cross the mountain backdrop, white wingbars blinking in the sun at every stroke, and in that moment another conviction of mine is tellingly reinforced: it is that the mountain experience begins far from the mountainside.

The birds have vanished. But the glasses which followed them now retrace their flightpath back across the moor until they home in on the two mountain summits. I have passed the end of the second shoulder and now the summits are locked into their

Stuc a' Chroin (left) and Ben Vorlich and the landscape clasp of the Bealach an Dubh Chorein

The moorland pedestal of Uamh Bheag, viewpoint for a painter

Nature as scene-shifter . . . Stuc a' Chroin emerges from behind lesser mountain shoulders

true places in the landscape, bridged by the bealach. I cling still to my north-eastering route, climbing steadily now until I have reeled in one more landmark. It is a less specific point on the landscape than either rock or green mound: I have climbed the slopes of Uamh Bheag in search of a viewpoint. What I want to find is a painting.

A month before, I visited an exhibition by Michael Andrews called 'Ayers Rock and Other Landscapes' at the Scottish National Gallery of Modern Art in Edinburgh. His Ayers Rock paintings had travelled before him thanks to a television programme, huge canvases of sensational colour, the blood red of the rock that bled down into the parched earth of the Australian bush, skies which almost hurt your eyes with their blueness. But television failed to convey the scope of the biggest paintings, the manner in which the rock thrust forward from the plane of the canvas, such was the artist's feel for the endless depths of that vast and parrot-bright landscape. But then there were the 'other landscapes'.

Cheek by jowl with the red earth and the wild kangaroos was a wide shallow canvas of a mountain skyline, a softer, greener realm that was at once both familiar and eerily strange because it had stepped, as it were, from the Australian outback. It was the mountain skyline of my own workaday world, my Scottish Southern Highland domain, with, at its heart, Ben Vorlich, Stuc a' Chroin and the Bealach an Dubh Chorein. The viewpoint was Uamh Bheag, a low and elegant hill where the artist's gaze had pierced the innards of Gleann an Dubh Chorein with its burn bisecting the landscape beneath the summits and burrowing at last into the crown of the bealach, the centre of the centre, a pure source of primeval life. It was a painting I might have stepped out of at any season of the year, so often have I wandered and climbed it. Its subject was so familiar in my life but the viewpoint quite new. Besides, the artist had elevated it to something exotic, a landscape of legend to be equated at the exhibition-goer's glance with Ayers Rock. Doubtless my Australian counterpart, should such a creature exist, might have stood in the midst of the same exhibition and knowing only the primary-coloured bravura of Ayers Rock would marvel instead at the soft green summer garb – and yes, the exoticness – of these home hills of mine.

It was a curious and oddly troubling hour for me. I have never hesitated to champion Scotland's mountain landscapes, believing they rank with the best of anyone else's, but somehow I had never considered that this one, with two of the three mountains I know best for a focal point (the third is Ben Ledi, two glens to the west and not in the picture), was in any sense among the elite. Now in the company of Michael Andrews's sensational portrayals of Ayers Rock, I was invited to treat my own landscape on that same elite level, and it emerged from my new scrutiny as precisely that, and I loved it the more. I studied the painting to see how he might have conferred additional and imaginary beauties, but if anything he had played down its impact by choosing to paint the whole in the untypical garb of August's softest green, and the work was faithful to all my familiarities of the mountains. He had, however, flung the ridges wide open by his choice of viewpoint, and it was that which gave them an air of mystery in my eyes, the familiar rendered unfamiliar by avoiding all the overlapping mountain shoulders which hamper most prospects into these mountains.

Long after I had left the gallery, the paintings still troubled me. It was hours later that I pinned down the source of my discomfort. It was that I, who watch the landscape to the extent that I write about it for a living, I who knew this of all landscapes to the extent of the very rock where a vole skull bleaches, I who value landscapes as others value religion in their lives (a spiritual rock to cling to), I had been seduced into reassessing the landscape significance of my own threshold because a famous artist had given it an exhibition context alongside an Australian rock. It is, to be sure, a particularly charismatic Australian rock, and many a Scot who could spin you a couple of coherent sentences about it could not stick a pin in a map of the Highlands within fifty miles of Stuc a' Chroin and Ben Vorlich. But I was left to ponder that my own familiarity with my nearest mountain skyline had bred in me a kind of landscape blindness. Had I found the skull of the vole and lost sight of the mountain?

So now, rearranging the mountains as I tread my north-eastering groove across the moor and up the slopes of Uamh Bheag on the headiest of autumn days, I seek out an unfamiliar viewpoint and a painting to step into, and I carry with me that unanswered question.

Uamh Bheag rises straight from the moor. On its steepest northern flank where the moor beneath has narrowed to a high wedge a quarter of a mile wide, what I remember of the painting falls into place, and so does a supreme irony. For this is early October, the sun is full on the mountains and the mountains are robed in the blaze shades of prime autumn. It is not the green mountains of Andrews's painting which sculpt the day's skyline but mountains which fuse his landscapes of two hemispheres into one – Ben Vorlich, Stuc a' Chroin and the Bealach an Dubh Chorein nature-painted the searing blood red and orange of Ayers Rock.

A long hour on the hillside: I watch the sun lower and force the shadowing stain of mountain shoulders ever deeper into the glens, while stags on every hill and moorland mile prowl and pester harems of hinds from handfuls to dozens, pouring the open-throated anthems of the red deer rut on the mountain air. The hour unlocks for me the manacles of over-familiarity, reaffirms in me the belief that in terms of an ambition to grow closer to nature there is no such thing as over-familiarity. I find that by scouring the memory of all my years in these hills for the indelible days and hours and moments, I have amassed a personal archive which has won viewpoints more telling than this, for I also know them from within. The view from the artist's seat reminds me that the Bealach an Dubh Chorein is much more than a mountain crossroads. It is also a bridge through half a lifetime, solidly founded on mountain truths, and in that high pass, that watershed, that launch pad for adventure and philosophy and eagles, is an idea called home.

'In so many ways the river is the glen — its voice, its focal point, its life force and its binding strength'

Chapter Six

'THE BEN IS SO HEALTHY . . .'

YOU COULD HARDLY call the glen beautiful, although there are beauties of a kind stashed away, unsung in secret places you unearth over years. It boasts no mountain worth drooling over through a camera viewfinder, although from its own unsung summits every compass point is distinguished by a sung one. The glen epitomises the low Highlands, an oasis in a mountain tumult. It has perhaps always been an introverting, turned-aside place, its own place. It certainly has that feel to it now, although for much of its story it was a place where folk would live and love and hate and work and hunt and sing and play and versify and die.

Often, when the restlessness of my life has cried out for a hill shoulder to lean on, it is to the glen that I have turned, to its unspectacular sense of self-containment, the more remarkable because of the mountainous company it keeps. However you reach the glen, you must travel through mightier realms by far, but a landscape which impresses with its tremendousness does not often impress with its tranquillity.

It is as if nature has made a space in the mountain midst and filled it with the glen. It achieves its tranquillity by its wide airiness, the way the hills lean back from the river as though out of respect, encouraging all the river's resonances. In so many ways the river *is* the glen – its voice, its focal point, its life force, its binding strength. Curiously for this part of the world, it is not even a mountain river. It is born, full of urge and surge in a loch to the north-east; it enters the glen in its second mile mature and amber as Glenlivet. Fifteen miles to the south-west it is lost to a second loch as if it had never been. There is no sweet-springing mountain source, no salt commingling with the sea. From loch to loch it falls not much more than 400 feet, and through the glen, barely 300. For much of its length it looks a benign water, but it wields a terrible power. It has an uncanny appetite for its fringing alders and hazels and birches, snatching one in the night as one-sidedly as a gale hurtles a finch east when it wants west.

There are other more blatant reminders of its power – rapids where the water rears like white stallions, breaks its own back, smashes the fragments down into its own irrefutable flow to rear again, the stallions restored. I have often watched canoeists tangle with the whitened river (intoxicated by the Glenlivet miles). I want to show them how the river works the stallion trick and shout above the shriek as the stallion spines disintegrate: 'Look, that's how it's done.'

My tent is well accustomed to a shelf of riverbank, my fire to mornings and evenings where sun and shadow roll up and down the hillsides like blinds, softening the smother of Commission forest which has been over-zealously done here. We know too ('We'? – tent and fire and I) those still and sodden daybreaks, the fire hissingly truculent, a pan of water all but unboilable. On such a day the sky is a lowered false ceiling on the glen's walls. Small slivers of cloud have snagged on rock face and treetop and the buzzard's falling note is the only fit anthem.

> Weep then tear-eager hill
> and spill soft threnody.
> Draw veils across
> tree-bartered peace
> cloud-smokily ill at ease.

> No deer shelter
> where no rain damps down
> twilit tree-cramped terrain.
> Who hears Fair Duncan now
> in the dripping drab?

Fair Duncan of the Songs, Duncan Ban Macintyre, knew these hillsides as few men can possibly have known them since, for he belonged to the latter end of that long and indefinable era of that older mountain order I invoked in Chapter One. He also immortalised that era uniquely and to those who know of him at all, it is as a Gaelic poet. His poetry is the voice of that race who lived within the mountain orbit and were comfortable there. Those who believe that men feared mountains before the Victorians kicked off the climbing boom and its tourist industry, have never reckoned with the eager intimacy of Beinn Dorain. Here is one who could say, as Sherpa Tenzing did of his own people years after Everest, 'We look at the mountain and we see ourselves. We are the blood. The mountain is the bone.'

Fair Duncan was born a few glens away from my shoulder-leaning place in 1724. His birthplace is a shameful monument now, a ruin among many township ruins and a cairn, the township all but inundated by one more thoughtless forest plantation. His great work, 'In Praise of Beinn Dorain', a long poem ingeniously shoe-horned into the formal rhythms and structure of pibroch, has long intrigued Gaelic scholars and there are several modern translations, notably one by Iain Crichton Smith. But I have a particular affection for the naive charm of a less familiar translation, for it was written by a friend, the late Albert Mackie, journalist, poet, playwright and much else besides, who died in his eighties a year or two after he walked into the office of the

Edinburgh Evening News (where I worked at the time) and handed me a signed copy of the unpublished manuscript. His gesture, and the conversation which followed, had sprung from many previous conversations during his weekly visits with copy for his column in the newspaper. Over three or four years we established a rare friendship. I was half his age when we met, but we found common ground on topics as diverse as football, the Highlands, the state of Europe, Edinburgh (which we both loved), the great writers of Scotland and Ireland. As he was leaving, he grasped my arm and with tears deepening his eyes he said, 'Ah, James . . . (he always called me James) . . . I knew the Artist when he *was* a Young Man.'

For a moment he was the great genius of literature he might have been had circumstances been kinder to him, then he was a mortal old man again who had to write an evening newspaper column to help to make ends meet. I watched him cross the office to leave, a slight and increasingly frail figure, scattering smiles and greetings at everyone from copy boys and girls to the editor; I marvelled at the man. I still do, and I keep a fond memory of him warm.

He knew his mountains too, and his Beinn Dorain is illumined by his own innate Highland-ness and he knew, too, a kinship of spirit with the legacy of Fair Duncan. Macintyre wrote nothing down, which makes his 550-line 'In Praise of Beinn Dorain' all the more conspicuous an achievement. As Marion Campbell wrote of him in her exquisite book *Argyll, the Enduring Heartland*:

> We are too apt to confuse literature with literacy as we are apt to look across such empty landscape as this and call it a wilderness. If one wants to be pedantic, the *filidh* of Celtic times was technically illiterate, or at least forbidden to use writing. He studied metres and exemplars during seven long years of training; how long must a man study when he has no tutor but his own ear and his own gift?

So allowing for mischiefs and misinterpretations on the part of those who did write it down (ministers mostly) and the freedom of the translator to create not just a translation but a poem in a different language more than 200 years after the event, it is to Albert Mackie's lasting credit that the whole thing works and serves well the cause of Scotland's one enduring mountain poet and the mountain landscape he so adored. In the following extract, 'the troop' is a herd of red deer, a dominant theme – Macintyre was a stalker.

> I loved to be watching
>   The troop smartly hustling
> Up the cliff of the Sroin
>   Ascending and bustling
> Up by Craobh na h-Ainnis
> And by Coire Dhaingein

The mountains of the Black Mount, birthplace of the poet Duncan Ban Macintyre

With heads held high thronging
    For handouts unpaid for;
Around Coire Rainich
And the flank of the Bealach,
Coire Reidh Beinn Ach-Chaladair
    And over by Connlon,
On Lurgan na Laoidhre
    They pass without longing,
By Larach na Feinne
And then by Creag Seileach,
Rank grasses disdaining,
    The hinds would go bounding.
'Twas their joy and their pleasure
To tread a gay measure
On pastures they'd treasure
    And moorland surrounding:
In airy pools prancing,
Excitedly dancing
And wildly advancing
    With cantrips astounding;
No thirst to torment them
When under Meall Tionail –
The water of Annad
    Is wine honey-flavoured,
A bright stream of virtues
That through the sand filters,
It's sweeter than cinnamon
    As we have savoured:
The physic enduring
Earth yields for their curing,
Their good health ensuring,
    Not purchased with money,
In folds of the mountain
With riches abounding,
Whose like won't be found in
    My quarter of Europe,
With such a pure fountain,
So tasty – clear-spouting,
The gentle, kind, bountiful
    Brew that is purest:
The bright water presses
Through dark roots of cresses

And varied moss dresses
    The verges and borders.
The clear-surfaced pool
Coming clean, sweet and cool
Through the gravelling mould
    On the shoulder of Dorain.
The Leacainn side's lovely
    With cover so pleasant,
The Frith-Choirean's rocky
    In contrast adjacent:
It's pillared and craggy
And knobbly and shaggy
And pitted and raggy
    And rugged and tufted
With dress rough and baggy
    Yet pretty and curly:
Its rough little passes
Are lush with tall grasses,
Its richness surpasses
    The tamer low country;
Bud-rich and clustered
    With slopes and plains marled,
With blooms clean and blushing
And many rich colours
And sweet green abundance
    The forest's apparelled.

It is a fitting and thoughtful analogy Marion Campbell draws, twinning the confusions of literature and literacy, and empty landscape and wilderness. Duncan Ban Macintyre wrote with the hand of nature, which is literacy enough. (Seton Gordon, whose books distinguished the literature of the Scottish landscape throughout the first half of the twentieth century, quotes the following: 'Donnachd Ban, who was under arms in the rising of 1745, was unable to read English, but one day when he was handed a newspaper by a brother soldier he was too proud to confess his ignorance. After a time the soldier who had lent him the paper exclaimed, "Duncan! It is the wrong end of the paper you have up!" Duncan, who had been holding the paper upside-down, promptly replied: "It does not matter which end is up, to a good scholar."')

Even allowing for the translator's free handling of the 200-year-old text of Beinn Dorain, there is no disguising the fact that the original was the fruit of a mind both fluent and ingenious, the work of a poet-scholar-mountaineer-naturalist whose intimacy with his subject stemmed from the fact that he knew it not as wilderness but as neighbourhood. It was the centrepiece of the landscape where he grew up, and in those years of his life when he worked as a stalker, it was where he earned his living, as back-of-the-hand familiar with his landscape as any taxi driver with his city streets.

If there is a single figure I could put a name to, representative of that earlier era from whom the throwbacks might have been handed down that sense of rightness regained which David Craig identified, it could perhaps be Duncan Ban Macintyre. Yet even he was probably among the last of that line. By the time he died in 1812, the map of the Highlands had changed irrevocably, damnably, and with it the Highland way of life. Prejudice and propaganda betrayed the Highlander and his landscape to those beyond the Highlands. He was reputedly surly and savage and illiterate. The landscape was miscalled and if it wasn't miscalled it was mightily misunderstood by so many eminent voices that it smacked of conspiracy. While Rousseau then Coleridge then Wordsworth were being moved to ecstasies by mountains in England, Dr Johnson was suffering the Highlands and Islands, scorning their 'wide extent of hopeless sterility' and Dickens found Glencoe 'perfectly terrible . . . such haunts as you might imagine yourself wandering in, in the very height and madness of a fever . . .'

The betrayal was just as blatant at government level, yet truth and enlightenment were all around them. The most elementary research condemned their mouths – say a study of that one remarkable poem or a walk with its author over what was an unremarkable and typical Highland mountain landscape. Remember?

> Its rough little passes
> Are lush with tall grasses
> Its richness surpasses
> The tamer low country . . .

Poem and landscape have two things in common: fertility and harmony. The fertility of the poet's mind is matched by the lushness of the landscape, a claim which must sound preposterous to the casual observer of today's Highland landscape. What Dr Johnson thought he saw has become reality, but only after 200 intervening years of enforced depopulation, ruthless deforestation and a cynical policy of land use based on sheep and deer. The deer, when they were a natural component in nature's scheme of things, were a part of the place, woodland beasts mostly, whose numbers were held in check by natural forces, notably wolves. The sheep were never a part of the place. Macintyre foresaw the devastation, and urged the hill fox to greater endeavour:

> My blessings with the foxes dwell
> For that they hunt the sheep so well.
> Ill fa' the sheep, a grey-faced nation;
> That swept our hills with desolation . . .

Beinn Dorain, the subject of Duncan Ban Macintyre's immortal masterpiece

OPPOSITE:
'. . . An offshoot of the main glen with a perfect raven-loud corrie hidden above the source of an exquisite burn. . .'

'In Praise of Beinn Dorain', written around 1776, is documentary evidence of a landscape in harmony, of flourishing deer, flowers, grass and native forest (not to be confused with the monoculture harvests which today's Highlands reap, another land use which, when it is overdone, inhibits human and wildlife populations and fosters a natural disharmony), mountains and people. If Duncan Ban Macintyre could see his beloved mountain now he would find it impoverished, his beloved forests conspicuous by their stunted remnants, his beloved red deer relegated to pot-shot playthings, over-populous and meagre, mediocre beasts compared to his prime stag:

> Coat beyond compare,
> Flag of radiant flare,
> Red as wax and rare . . .

As for the land itself, two lines confound the conspirators:

> In herbs and in verdure
> The ben is so healthy.

The fact that the conspiracy did its work devastatingly well, the fact that the land is in poorer health now than it has ever been . . . these do not mean that I do not love the glen as I find it now, nor that I am inhibited in my efforts to grow close to it. It is still a beautiful place, nature is still the predominant force, Beinn Dorain is still a supreme mountain. But to grow close to the place now is not the same thing as Duncan Ban Macintyre's closeness. He would wear the mountain garb because he was born to it, because he was of that era which lived in the mountain's orbit and was comfortable there. I must put on the mountain garb each time I go and the closeness only comes at the height of the longest contemplative stillnesses I can muster. You must clutch at echoes and do what I like doing least – go back. If you would sense the bond between man and landscape (which, whether acknowledged or not, is at the root of even today's commercially callous exploration of our mountains), then you must unfetter your mind and let it roam amid Fair Duncan's landscapes and beyond, back into the heyday of wolf and bear, lynx and beaver, and high and wide miles of pine and birch and oakwood, for they all thrived here or hereabouts. Listen to what you hear. Acknowledge that when the Highlands were well populated by their own folk, wildlife and wild woodland thrived and a poet could call a mountain healthy.

On a flank of a small cul-de-sac, an offshoot of the main glen with a perfect raven-loud corrie hidden high beyond the source of its exquisite mountain burn, I pause beside a newly cut drainage ditch. The plough has exhumed the bones of ancient trees, embalmed in peat, twisted as frayed old rope, smooth as peach skin to the touch. I sit to listen and go back. I uncork the hipflask and raise it to the unborn generations of trees which the conspirators have denied us.

THE BEN IS SO HEALTHY

Scent the distilled essence
of the land; scan the sheep-shorn glen;
toast the woodland that was not.

Drink:

To every willow
which never wept
with the joy of being.

To every silver birch
which never found
its crock of gold
at summer's rainbow's end.

To every rowan
which never bannered
the throneroom of an eagle
and to every eagle eyrie
never built
and every eaglet
which never fledged
and never flew
from a rowan-bright nursery.

To every hazel
oak and aspen
which never shadowed the burn
and every trout and salmon
which never lingered
in pools never shaded.

To every songbird
which never pierced
every silent May-Day dawn
and never lived to die
in the fast clutch
of every sparrowhawk
never weaned in nests
which never leaned
by tall pine trunks
which never grew

in the woodland that was not.

To every tree-creepering
woodpeckering owl-hootering thing
which never clawed bark
which never wrapped
all the ungrown woodlands
and every roe deer and stoat
badger and bat squirrel and wildcat
four-legged this-and-that
which never stepped
into woodland clearings
across the whole unwooded hill.

To every woodland moth
and mite and moss
and tree-thirled lichen
which never sought a tiny haven here.

A health to you
wherever you prospered.
It was not here
on the hill grown empty
as a hollow tree.

I do not much like to 'go back', partly because in Scotland today, going back seems to have become a national disease. Politically, for example, the land has become convinced that the golden age ended the day before yesterday. I do not believe it. Historically, there has always been another golden age, but the worst vantage point to see its approach is the throes of depression. When I sit on the glen's hillside and force my mind back it is to tell myself where I came from. It is to sense the land when it was healthy, that above all other things. If the only way to taste the land in its prime is to go back, so be it, but it serves its purpose only if that taste stimulates a new determination to win back the health of the land.

It is not a dewy-eyed quest. The health of the mountain land is achievable, given the two essentials of Duncan Ban Macintyre's poem: fertility and harmony. Fertility is achievable, but not under existing land use systems. The day of the big estates is almost done. When the sun finally sets on it, there will be no louder cheer than mine. With a few honourable exceptions, it has proved an oppressive, self-centred and destructive regime, draining the land of its people, its wildlife, its woods and moors and meadows, its health. One of the most fertile and wooded glens of which Duncan

Ban Macintyre would have knowledge must have been Glencoe. Look at the legacy of two centuries of estate management there and shudder.

Fertility can be won back. Harmony will follow, for it means nature and landscape and people working towards a balance by which they can all thrive. We cannot achieve the specific harmony which Fair Duncan and his predecessors would have known, for we have changed as much as the land. Yet we can learn from old harmonies. What were their priorities? How did they control the health of the land, how contribute to it? Land reform must be our starting point. Widespread expansion of the crofting model would assist the return of people, fertility, wildlife and health to the land, and once our red deer numbers have been halved and there is a government commitment in place to keep them that way, there is really no need for anyone to own land above 2000 feet.

When you go and sit alone on your hillside with the headstones of a dead wood at your feet, the moss-furred blurs of old shielings half a mile upstream, the once 'so healthy' ben grazed to the bone, and a 200-year-old poem in your head, it is not hard to see how much is lost. If you do not yearn for change you are either a sheep, a rock, a foreigner, a politician, or a landowner.

Go and sit on a hillside and listen and look and go back. See the evidence of the conspiracy, sense the land when it was healthy, scent the wind of change which must blow to bear the cure. We have grown too suspicious of summer here. We think of winter as our natural season, when the whole landscape pares to the bone like the mountain, when we can turn up our collars and go before oppressive winds in a nationalistic crouch. I suffer from it myself. When I worked through my photographs to make a selection for this book I noticed how many of them show the mountains in snow, how few in summer's brief green. Yet it was in this same glen of all places I wrote this:

> The summer pool lips gingerly
> slips lingeringly through
> its sunken, shrunken chamber
> below the fall
> the fall which merely stumbles
> now, barely taking the trouble
> to whiten. The memory of winter
> spates' brutality's beyond recall.
>
> A wren lodged in a hazel
> like a nut
> flings shining semi-quavers
> across the tree's fattening
> shortening shadow.
> It's all too poised

AMONG MOUNTAINS

too pipit-polite
too dripping green
for my winter addiction
– but oh! I taste
that dawdling scented summer air
thyme after thyme.

Chapter Seven

THE KILLER

I WATCHED THE postman empty a fistful of bills through my letterbox. I let them lie on the floor for a few minutes wondering if that sinister little litter could possibly conceal some good news, a cheque even? I could imagine none, and rose from the typewriter to gather the mail. I was wrong. Among that spoilheap of bureaucracy there was an envelope typed in the distinctive style I had come to associate with Mike Tomkies. It is difficult to imagine a time now when we were not friends, but it is only a dozen years since we first met. The letter, in the spring of 1985, contained an invitation. It is fair to say that it played a significant part in changing the course of my life.

Mike Tomkies is a *great* wildlife writer. I choose the adjective with care. Over the past twenty-five years he has produced a unique body of work championing the cause of rare wildlife and wild places, much of it in Scotland. He has done it the hard way, trekking thousands of miles, watching for thousands of hours, living a life closer to nature than most people have dared for 200 years, since the day of Fair Duncan of the Songs, perhaps.

We met after I had reviewed his book *Between Earth and Paradise*, and although I was still plying my journalist's trade then, we unearthed enough common ground to form the basis of what has become a valued and enduring friendship. In its early years, his letters offered both generous encouragement in my writing endeavours and tantalising glimpses into his West Highland world. Twice I trekked the six trackless lochshore miles to the isolated cottage he called Wildernesse, learning a little more each time, about Mike, about the worth of wildness, about eagles especially, for there are few people alive who know more about them than he does. I was still trying to fathom him out at that stage: most loners are complex characters who tend to tolerate visitors only if they respect territory and ritual, but once I had made it clear that I respected and valued both, his hospitality was warm and generous, and it has been ever since. He reminded me a little of a wolf, for his loyalty to his place and his wild kin were both unswerving and touching. Early reservations were soon brushed aside by a growing admiration for his work and total lack of compromise. I never met another

Wildlife writer and photographer Mike Tomkies at work with camouflaged telephoto lens and hide

The golden eagle eyrie cliff at the far end of the trek Mike Tomkies calls the Killer. (Photo Mike Tomkies)

human more attuned to the element of wild nature, nor one who dwelt more *appropriately* among mountains. Fair Duncan would have approved, I am sure, though Mike Tomkies is more philosopher than poet.

I wrote a newspaper piece about one of those early treks. I remembered that he accompanied me part of the way back along the lochside as I was leaving, and that after we had said our farewells I stopped again and turned to watch him walk back alone to the most isolated house I have ever encountered. It seemed then, as he returned, a loose fragment of that immense landscape had been put back into place. I still think of him that way, a man who is fit company for the eagles he so loves.

I opened the letter. The first paragraph contained the exciting news that his favourite eagle had a chick on her furthest eyrie. He called her Atalanta, a huge dark female, and spoke the name with a kind of awed reverence, not just once, but every time I heard it over a dozen years. He introduced her to the world in his book *Golden Eagle Years*:

> She was moving like some ethereal goddess of the aerial chase, and in that brief moment I thought of a good name for her – Atalanta, after the fleet mythical Greek goddess of the Calydonian Hunt who, as is also true in the eagle world, could outdistance and more than had the measure of any male of her species!

After the news came the invitation:

> Now, if you want an eagle weekend you could help me with cine gear and hide to Ata's nest! The sooner the better! If you could come this Friday, we could hike over early Saturday morning, put up hide, I could stay in it overnight and try to get 24 hours of good obs. We would then have to take the hide down as it's on an estate I am not sure of (as regards attitude to eagles) and I would not want anyone else to find it or use it. I can more or less guarantee you seeing eagles at least! . . . Don't walk in, I can meet you . . . This will save you the long hike in as you'll need your legs for the hike with hide and cine gear. It's a fair trek but between the two of us it won't be too bad . . .

'It's a fair trek'. I look at the words before me now as I write, and I shudder. It is the one Mike called 'the Killer Trek', an accolade I put down to a quirk of his writing style when I first heard him use it. He renamed his landscape – 'Eagle Rock Mountain', 'Guardian Mountain', 'Big Corrie' and so on – to cloak its identity. Killer Trek, I thought, is probably nothing more than a monument to a bad day. Ha!

We had, as I remember it, a shade too much whisky the night before to be in the best of fettle for a dawn push, and we sat through breakfast looking morosely at the rain. Still, it was May and the long Highland day was at our disposal. By late morning we were ready and the weather had relented just enough to be encouraging. Come on, Killer, do your worst. It began to do that at once. The trek began with the best part of 1000 feet of mountainside which reared behind the cottage. We gasped for breath and forswore drink forever. Between us we carried more than 80 lbs of gear, and I might have ventured a protest were it not for Mike's frequent expressions of gratitude. As if our packs were not heavy enough, progress was compounded by the fact that between us we carried the unwieldy hazel wands and netting for the hide. That meant that we had to walk not just at the same pace, but with the same rhythm and, as often as possible, on the same level. I remember with some gratitude of my own reaching the first level terrace on the first slope.

The high miles cross a sodden, tussocky plateau-ish mountain shoulder at a shade over 2000 feet. I crossed it that day thinking: 'This must be a phenomenal place on a good day.' We had entered the kind of situation I love on a mountain trek, a high, more or less level plateau surrounded by summits. The sense of an arena, a coliseum among mountains, is irresistible, we the suffering gladiators to entertain an audience of summits. The weight on our backs, the warm wet weather which soaked both outside and in, the awkwardness of the ground, the clumsy burden of the hide which pained our arms mercilessly, even the knowledge that the crux of the trek was still to come . . . all that might have lined a wild heart with lead. But the overwhelming sensation was one of privilege: I had been plucked from my Edinburgh newspaper office and elevated overnight to the status of first assistant to a champion of golden eagles! Now we crossed the roof of his realm, and as we walked and sweated and swore at each stumble and sodden gust or called a halt to change hands on the end of the rolled-up hide's poles, I was suddenly aware again that I was in the company of a fragment of nature, a piece of the landscape.

The world began to tilt, gently at first, but from the absence of land immediately ahead, we were heading for an abyss of sorts. The 'sort' in question was the one which earned the trek its killer epithet. We were standing on top of a wall, not quite vertical but something perilously close to it, and one which was about to lose us almost every one of the 2000 feet we had climbed. We looked at the hide, at the wall which we must now descend, and reached an instant and unanimous decision. With three back-and-forward arm-swings to build up momentum we hurtled the hide into the void, and as it careered, bounced and rollicked down the wall, we set off after it. Every few minutes we caught it up where it had snagged on a shelf or a boulder, and we threw it again, and in that bizarre and brutal fashion we climbed down to the floor of the glen. I have never seen such a steep hillside which wasn't bare rock, and apart from the wall on the far side of the glen which had all the hallmarks of this one but climbed over 1000 feet higher, I was quite unfamiliar with such an unrelenting slog.

We recomposed the hide at the burn, drank lustily, pitied our knees, then set off on the trek's final mile, a new climb of 1000 steepening feet to the eyrie cliff, a toilsome plod up the flank of a buttress with a Gaelic name meaning 'level ground'! I have long suspected the Gael of exercising an ironic humour in the naming of his landscape. I can see some weary map-maker trudging this glen in the company of a local hird, having the features named and meticulously spelled out to him, the local growing more and more exasperated with his Sassnnach tongue and slipping in the odd piece of nonsense which was just as dutifully copied. From such moments, our landscape has acquired names like 'The Lochan of the Corrie of the Lochan', or so I choose to believe.

We climbed hard under the cliff face. During one brief pause I turned to take stock of my surroundings. For the first time I saw the mountain wall we had just descended, and for the first time it sank in that within a couple of hours I would have to climb it again. I shuttered the thought from my mind and concentrated instead on the sheer elemental wildness of my surroundings. You could not say that such a place was beautiful, for it's a crowding, powerful landscape of huge, blunt gestures, and in a restless light and a big wind, the buttresses and mountain walls and cliffs and glen floors switch off and on, light and dark and vivid and dull, and the wind and the falling waters underscore every shift and shade. It is not beautiful, then, but it thrills.

Fanfares and anthems would have been fitting finales for such a trek, but instead a thin, weedy cheep announced journey's end. We were under the eyrie and the eaglet was announcing our presence with no great enthusiasm.

I stared at the thing, an incongruous and unpretty mix of white fluffball and sturdy defiance. The yellow cere and hookbeak and hooded eye had all the hallmarks of eagle, but it was its birthplace which so impressed me. To be born *here*, into all this, to imbibe it naturally as you imbibe air, to grow learning mastery of its winds and, in time, to mark out a portion of it in your mind for your home territory, to climb a mile high on the best days and tilt the whole mountain mass in your eye with a langorous dip of wing, to carve through its air so that your thrown shadow is the most feared and respected thing in the land . . . in that confused and confusing moment I understood finally my companion's passionate pursuit of golden eagles, his relentless and unquenchable thirst to know more about them, to get closer to them, closer, perhaps than any man had been before. In the night that followed, Mike would register his 1000th hour in a hide watching eagles.

There will always be much that we will never know about such an uncompromising and unconfiding bird as a golden eagle, but Mike Tomkies has won remarkable insights into their world, and graced the literature of the Hill in the process. This is how you do it. You slog for years, for thousands of miles, for 1000 watching hours, and when your mind and body tell you, 'Never again', you draw on something else, some reserve drawn from nature, perhaps, and you get up and go and slog again.

Now we had to work fast. The whole object of the exercise was to put a hide in place which the eagles could not detect, put Mike in it with his cine gear; then I was to leave, fast and loud and as conspicuously as possible. The theory is that the eagle does not count, but registers only the presence of the intruder, its arrival and departure. Mike's hide-building technique is a marvel of camouflage. He describes the technique, and this whole trek, in his book, *Last Wild Years*.

> I worked from inside, forcing the ends of the three thick hazel poles into the earth, while Jim passed through the long slim bracers which I threaded in and out of the netting to make a rigid tunnel. After fixing on the sprigs of heather that we had

Eaglet on the Killer eyrie . . . one of many fine studies from the camera of Mike Tomkies

Atalanta, the golden eagle, photographed by Mike Tomkies, who named her after a Greek goddess

plucked on the way, we had nothing else with which to camouflage the hide but white tussock grasses. Like badgers, we clawed heaps of it from all over the area, weaving it quickly into the netting, and in less than an hour the hide was completely covered with natural vegetation and moss.

My last task before I left was to conceal the protruding telephoto lens with grasses, then, reassuring Mike that I would be very careful with his Calor-gas cooker, and not blow up his cottage, I stomped off downhill, singing, waving my arms and a white plastic carrier bag, anything to draw attention to my departure. I was buoyed up by the vigour of the past hour, setting up the hide, watching the eaglet, getting Mike installed, and being a part of the mountain world and its eagles. I sprang cheerfully down the hillside to the river. Then I stopped and looked up.

There is a psychology I bring to bear for such occasions. It works something like this: two hours from now this mountain wall will be behind you and you will be crossing the high arena, relishing every step, working alone, and in your element; better still, you will have earned it, because you will have climbed this monster; two hours . . . nothing at all, think back two hours and see how much you have accomplished in that time. So I kicked into the hillside and began, and so did the rain.

I had already thought a great deal about that part of the weekend, the solo trek back to Mike's cottage. I had to ensure that I pinned down every last vivid detail, for it was no meagre insignificance with which I had been entrusted, crossing unfamiliar mountains, looking after the cottage all night, then returning the next day to help Mike out, and all of it so that he could add to his film of the kind of wildlife I loved. I thought again how much I admired the way the man went about his business. That, I told myself as I trudged and clawed and cursed my way up the wall, was why I was here. In practice, I remember next to nothing about the trek. The rain closed in, the tops were smothered in cloud, and halfway across the arena, I began fantasising about a bottle of banana milk I had left in the cottage. When I finally found the burn that tumbles down to Mike's lochside wood, I was fit for nothing. The milk tasted like nectar. I stripped off, dried myself down, clambered into my sleeping bag for an hour at eight p.m. and woke up at three a.m. Meanwhile, at the far end of the Killer Trek . . .

I felt I must be mad. I had desperately wanted to spend my birthday with the eagles, a whole day-and-night stint, for this would certainly be the last time. It had been a 'killer' trek all right, and even with Jim's help I had carried more weight than ever. I was knackered before I got into the hide. Now I faced all night and most of the next day in this desolate place and in this awkward position.

It became bitter cold as dusk fell. Rain lashed down and leaks sprang all over the hide. The sleeping bag began to get wet and for the first time I felt panic. I might not survive this night at all and Jim would come back, if he *could* come back with the mountain tops drowning in mist, and find my cold body!

Last Wild Years spells out just what Mike went through that night, and it is his story rather than mine. I recommend it thoroughly to anyone who values our wild places and the wildest of our wildlife, or anyone who envies the lifestyle of a writer-naturalist. It bears repeating that if you would do such work, and if integrity is to be your first commandment, this is what it takes.

I lay in my sleeping bag listening to the rain playing paradiddles on the tin roof, and dozed no more than fitfully between three and eight a.m., when I gave up and rose to make breakfast. It was then I realised I hadn't eaten since a sandwich lunch somewhere on the trek yesterday. The banana milk was half drunk and in the morning light its pale yellow colour looked as unappetising a brew as I could imagine. I was stiff and sore, but my night had been warm and dry and restful. Mike's was cold, sodden, sleepless, endless in 'a claustrophobic trap', and in the perverse psychology which can overwhelm you in such extremes of circumstance he had to fight off panic and fear of death. But by four a.m. he was filming the eagles again, and in the late morning he produced some of his best eagle sequences and concluded:

> Well, a truly great morning, ranking with the best hours . . . After all the troubles,
> determination had paid off and I had the vital feeding sequence I wanted. I told myself
> I could leave Scotland with honour if I chose.

There was a blink of sunlight on the lochshore and I sat outside the cottage with my breakfast tea. The arrangement had been that I would return at about half-past three, but it became difficult to kick my heels for an extra hour, and I had the feeling Mike might appreciate my turning up early, after such a night . . .

. . . I paused at the river to drink, the wretched wall behind me. I scanned the facing slope trying to pin down the hide, but it was quite invisible. A piece of the mountainside suddenly seemed to dislodge, perhaps 300 feet above. It did not fall, but moved clear of the wall and a ripple went through it, an uncanny motion that seemed to buoy the thing on the air. Baffling moments passed while I puzzled over the shape, like a fish with a hump, then it canted over on its side and showed me a pair of dark eagle wings as big as doors. I had never seen such a giant, and guessed at once that I was looking at Atalanta, and knew at once why Mike Tomkies searched among the goddesses to name her. She came down the air towards me, yapped twice in that inconsequential voice of eagles, passed across my bows at 100 yards with her head cocked and sidelong, assessing my threat, then with her wings set in a glide, she devoured the glen at a barely believable speed. Mike has measured such 'jet glides' at more than 100 miles per hour. I watched her until she was too small to see, and in her going I knew another reason for being here, doing this. The Scottish mountain landscape is my own chosen realm too, and an eagle such as Atalanta is its finest ambassador. When the eagle is in good heart, the Highland landscape will be too.

I was twenty yards from the hide before I could see it, so well had its architect designed it, even if it was a sodden claustrophobic trap. I called out 'Mr Tomkies? I've come to read your electricity meter.'

But there was no answering laugh or greeting, just a fraught 'Thank Christ you're here.' Mike emerged stiff and frozen and almost blue. It had been a traumatic stint. Then the story poured out in half-formed sentences and exclamations, the ordeal punctuated with the highs of superb filming sequences. Mike remembers the moment thus:

> Never before had I been so pleased to hear a human voice. I had dreaded trying to carry all that gear back over the killer hill, if I could move my frozen legs at all. I took the camera down and tried to crawl out. It was impossible to move much faster than a sloth. The legs still worked but stiffly, slowly, like those of some long-buried ghoul emerging from a frozen tomb in a horror film.

We left the hide hidden away from prying eyes under a far cliff face, 'a gift to the mountain Gods', Mike said, and eased down to the river groaning under our heavy packs. I told Mike about the banana milk to try and lighten the moment, but all I got was a rebuke for not eating properly, which is probably what I would have done had the positions been reversed.

The wall had a curious effect on us. It was the fourth time I had negotiated it in twenty-four hours, and although I plugged well enough up the lower slopes, it finally did for me about three-quarters of the way up, and the last haul over false ridges was red-eyed agony, compounded by heavy rain.

But it seemed to liberate Mike. He was alive. He could savour the joy of movement. The ordeal had served its purpose. By the time we reached the plateau, he was well ahead, and then he began to jog! I thought 'He's twenty years older than me, he's had no sleep, he's spent the night in a grass coffin 1000 feet up a mountain in a downpour, he's got more than thirty pounds on his back, and now the bugger's jogging.'

I decided if he could, I could. I couldn't. Instead I stopped dead and yelled. Mike wrote in *Last Wild Years*:

> Halfway through Big Corrie Jim yelled for a breather. I turned round and saw him looking like a drowned beaver, swaying on his feet, even his powerful frame vulnerable. No doubt I looked worse. Jim had done that trek twice in twenty-four hours, something I had never done, and only to help me; I felt ashamed of my selfishness and apologised.

Such is the nature of the man. After the kind of night he had endured, I found his gesture quite touching. I willed one more effort out of my weary legs and pushed on into the rain, the mist, until the knee-jarring last steep slopes down to the cottage came into view and we could file the whole phenomenal expedition away into an honoured place in our personal anthologies of mountain-going. We washed, dried, changed, fed and watered heartily and relived those last two days until we were too tired to talk.

I drove home the next day believing life had turned a corner. The path which I had contemplated for so long seemed suddenly free from the strewment of rocks which had fankled progress. I believed I had things to say about nature and the Scottish landscape which had not been said and a way of saying them which had not been articulated. But all I had produced at that point was a collection of essays which had interested a couple of publishers but not interested them enough. I realised now that I was not aiming high enough. What was missing was the uncompromising slog and the integrity. It would take three more years before I left my newspaper job to write my books, but by then the slog had begun and I had a contract from Mike's publisher (to whom he had introduced me) for a book on the Cairngorms, *À High And Lonely Place*. The book was published in 1991, but the process of writing it began high on a mountainside far from the Cairngorms six years before, that mountainside which Mike Tomkies named (with slightly mischievous understatement worthy of his Gaelic blood) Big Corrie. Mike's practical example provided the extra motivation I needed. A week after our Killer Trek, he provided me with just a little extra, in one more letter:

> What a weekend of trekking! I am writing to thank you yet again for all the great help you gave me. I am sure without that help, Jim, I would never have got that huge double hide over the 'killer trek' along with all the cine gear as well and never got that superb stuff on May 25/26 on the eagles. Nor would I have gone back, as I did alone this weekend too, and got superb stuff of the male flying in and leaving the eyrie . . . these were the main sequences I needed to complete my eagles-at-the-nest material. I got it thanks to you. I did a twenty-four hour stint . . . the hide is back where we hid it . . . I fear it will remain there, as a sacrifice to the wild Gods of the eagle glen, for I doubt I will ever do that trek again . . .

He had gone back!
    Again.
    Alone.
    The one more time it was needed to complete the job, and that too is the nature of the man. For all my writing work among mountains from that May of 1985 until now, the killer trek has been my watershed and my yardstick and my motivator whenever I need an added impetus to go back one more time, and one more. I hope it will always be that way.

Chapter Eight

THE COE

THE COE HAS been good to me. I've had my soakings, my storm-tongue-lashings – who hasn't who climbs there often? – but I have had more than my share of the golden days there too: dawdles on frozen windless snow to the summit of Bidean, the Aonach Eagach when the pinnacles were warm to the touch, solitary treks up out of Leac na Muidhe over the slim ridges of the second-division mountains – Aonach Dubh a' Ghlinne and Beinn Maol Chaluim via the Bealach Fionghaill, mountains which might be famous were it not for the fact that they are wedged between Bidean and Starav. And some of the best days have been nights.

April is a knife-edge month in Glencoe. Spring in the sense of a greening of the land and the few trees which still cling on, is still a month away, perhaps two in a bad year of late frosts. But the meadow pipits are irreversibly thirled to their breeding season, free-falling down small chutes of song to a perch in the pale grasses or a cold stance on a boulder. In the black bosom of the Three Sisters, the raven is on eggs, the buzzard builds. And for the legions addicted to that matchless throng of mountains, the evening lengthens and the darkening mountains of dusk are to be relished, not feared, as they are in the worst winter depths.

The rockhounds have gone from Stob Coire an Lochain to the Clachaig's fire. The corrie is empty, the lochan shore still, the water the palest shade of blue you would not call white. The Aonach Eagach across the Coe is a shade I wouldn't dare put a name to, something between gray and orange. I have had a brew by the lochan, and put a splash of burn water in a hip-flask dram. I have simply no interest in going down. The burn is in good voice. A raven is talking to itself, and answers its own echo. These are all the conversation I need. The promise of a full moon is broken by a trap-door of cloud which inches quietly through the glen from the west, closes neatly on every summit. For an hour there is something like darkness, then the moon gains in confidence and begins to infiltrate the cloud from above. There is no moonlight, at least not the kind that throws shadows, but it lightens the cloud to an off-white night and the mountain shapes stand perfectly defined. There is light enough in the corrie to climb or descend, or stay put. Climbing again, back up to the day's summit, seems pointless now. The only purpose in a summit at night is a moonlit panorama, but the cloud base is 500 feet too low for that. Staying put has become too cold for comfort. Perhaps descent then? I know a place . . .

. . . The house is a corpse now. You could say much the same of the glen: the living has all but gone, likewise the fields, woods, children, old ones, music. The house knew them all. Now it knows the stench and shit of sheep.

It was a small single-storey house, and it was dark. All houses were dark then. What good was light in a house? The more light that got in, the more weather did too. If you built such a house in such as Glencoe, you built so that the weather was not an invited guest. If there was a single window, it was small and deep-set, and the small table stood there. It was a bard's place, I think. The small window was light enough for composing bardly things. It seems strange, a house in such a place and no way to let the mountain view in? If you want to look at the mountains, said its builder, go and stand at the open door. There is light and there are mountains enough beyond the door without bringing them in. Well, they are in now, alright. How long since the roof was torched?

It is not admirable, the way the house is now. What's admirable in a corpse? But admire the walls. See how the corners are round? They were not cut that way, but there are round cornerstones a-plenty in the river. A round corner silences the wind, so that it blows by as unheard as it is unseen. And because the walls are broken, you can see the double thickness. Between the outer and inner walls was a third wall of turf. The wind was never born which could breach such defences. And you thought cavity-wall insulation was a new thing! The turf was thick on top of the walls too, for the roof fitted inside them. No scope there for winds either, and the wall-top was a walkway for the roof repairers. It was a good house. It still is, and it gives my sleeping bag a good wind-break. It is not my intention to sleep (although the occasional half-hour doze is a welcome break from a night of watching and listening to the mountains), but to keep the company of the old stones, perhaps divine some sense of place, a hint of the particular mountain closeness which must have attended every aspect of human life here in the throwback days. There is a working farm across the river, but it is hard by the main road, and about as far as it is possible to get in that neck of the Pass of Glencoe from the mountains, which, admittedly, is not far. But the ruin is below the farm and out of sight of the road, hard by the river with its infinite varieties of speech, and so close to the blackened terraces of the Three Sisters that there are fast-skied moments when they seem to tremble and step forward and withdraw and dance above your head.

Now, at three a.m., under that moon-white, summit-clogging sky, the buttresses are overbearing, and look like unconnected mountains. It is not fear, exactly, which they impart, but this is a place for a clear head and a steady nerve. Whoever lived here must have learned a very specialised kind of acclimatisation, or perhaps they were born to it, already acclimatised, and went uneasily beyond the mountain shadows.

The ruined bard's cottage in Glencoe at first light . . . 'I am looking for a hint . . . what it was like to wake here . . .'

The high corrie of Stob Coire an Lochan above the unmistakable V of the Pass of Glencoe

There are few night sounds above the continuous undertones and overtones of the river. The owl's voice is a surprise. It comes from somewhere down past the Clachaig on the old road to the village, distant and unrelated to this treeless airt. I resume trying to separate the river's speech into distinct tongues: the chatter over shallows, the gurgling deeps, the six-inch fall among boulders, the prickly meander of a side-stream among pebbles, that kind of thing. All the while I stare up at Aonach Dubh, Gearr Aonach, occasionally to the brutish night-glower of the Bodach hung high on the gibbet of the glen's far wall. But after about ten minutes of half-an-ear listening I have grown interested in the owl, for it sounds as if it has crossed the river now. The calls grow louder until they are palpably a part of the cottage's landscape. I don't remember an owl in Glencoe before, but as I have spent no more than a couple of dozen nights in the glen, it is perhaps not surprising. Besides, nothing sharpens your appreciation of night sounds like being a fragment of the wakeful night, not shut out of it in tent or bunkhouse or hotel, but open to it. Now I have tuned in to the owl, trying to place it as it calls. It is a tawny owl's voice heading ever deeper into a landscape ever more starkly opposed to its preferred woody realm. Perhaps it too is a throwback yearning after a handed-down instinct of the glen as a wooded place.

There is a lull. I hear above the river these sounds: a trickle of stones on a restless mountain flank, a bellow of sheep, a truck (a night-blind imposter using headlights to see), an oyster-catcher piping past, a mouse in the cottage grass. Then suddenly the owl is on the gable, a vole in its foot. At my wordless gasp it rises again, banks halfway across the living-room, crosses the low wall and is gone. Its sounds were the braking rasp of wings, the scrape of a talon on the stone, the rush of air through the widest panache of spread wings as the bird banked. The darkness offered up the owl; the darkness reclaims the owl, and for minutes afterwards I sit rigid with raw fright. Had I been a Glencoe vole, I would have died of a heart attack before the talon bit and crushed.

The night fades, not paling so much as withdrawing its blackness, so that the hidden gray beneath is revealed. There is an hour before six a.m. when the gray hovers and infiltrates every niche and shadow, ousting night and blackness. Even the great buttresses pale to it.

A meadow pipit stirs, rises, opens its throat, marks out its unseen slide down the air, then falls down it, cock-tailed and singing. The free-fall ends on the owl's gable. The bird surveys me at the far end of my red sleeping bag, smirks 'No bad, eh?', and flickers away. There are other songs to sing, chutes to slide down, mates to win. Within minutes I can hear or see six sliding pipits, and the morning is confirmed. I stow the sleeping bag and go out to join the pipits.

The cottage is an old haunt of mine and I had found it easily enough in the midnight darkness, its walls showing stubbornly against the moon-paled clouds. Now, though, I wanted to watch it waken. I waded the river (the upstream bridges are an abomination and have no place here; they are there because the National Trust for Scotland broke and continues to break the rules under which it was obliged to manage

Glencoe). From the far bank I could look at the cottage from below, setting it against the buttresses, or against the climbing, funnelling length of the main glen.

I am looking for something – what? I don't know, a hint, a happening, an insight – which will let me in on what it was like to wake here, to step out of your door and be as familiar with the dawn mountains as you are with your garden. Not *these* mountains, of course, but the Glencoe of that earlier mountain order to which the cottage belongs. It should be easy here (and *now* in the first light of this early April morning with Glencoe knife-edged on the faded night of winter and the dawn of spring), easy to don the cloak of the mountain quiet and peel back the layers of intervening centuries which shaved the landscape to its skin and covered the tracks of the Glen folk. It should be, but it is not.

All the raw materials are in place. This was a community of bards. These very stones which have sheltered me and pillowed my head and fleetingly accommodated the successful owl, the breathless pipit . . . here is a *bard's* home. Here, perhaps, the doings of MacIain, the Old Fox, were told and foretold:

> The Snow is on the Land like a shroud. I have never seen such wreathings. The Old Ones, those who still see with the eyes of the Storm, are full of warnings. MacIain, they say, is at that dangerous age where he is too old to lead us with the clarity of the Eagle's vision, yet not old enough to see with the eyes of the Storm.
>
> Not even the cunning of the Old Fox is immune to the gray dulling of his eye.
>
> But I dare not write such things, not in my songs and poems and heroic accounts. I secrete them into this locked journal which others may unearth when the Shroud and the Death-mask of this glen are peeled back by a kindlier spring. The truths they will learn are written first in the Mountains and copied by my hand according to what I am told and what I can read.

It was from these stones that I wrested a character for a one-woman play, *Woman of Glencoe*, in 1990, a bard charged with interpreting a vision relayed by a mountain God, in the bleak February of 1692.

> I have known all this for some time, for I have read of it in the usual places. The Mountains and all Nature are my sources. Today I saw a new sign, MacIain's wife shawled in a shadow. Her eye was a hood.
>
> MacIain too is marked, but I have known that since the mountain threw a swan shape of cloud on the Glen and I watched the wild swans which winter on Loch Achtriochtan. Yet this has been such a hard winter that the swan-wanderers should have moved on, south to Forth or Solway. Instead they stayed. I have learned to read from such signs of Nature. They stayed daring the icing of the loch, the snows, weakening, until by the year's end the male bird was dead. That marked MacIain, for I say the swan was a harbinger, sent by his death to warn Glencoe. But who heeds me now? Keep your darkness to yourself, pagan hag, they say. MacIain has troubles

The Pap of Glencoe . . . 'it is not conservation Glencoe needs but a cure . . .'

OPPOSITE: *The cottage under its mountain . . . a withered bloom of the true glen*

enough. It is the scriptures you should scan for your truths, not the Mountains, they tell me. Yet it was not the Scriptures which sent the swans.

Last night I found the dead swan's mourning mate sick and dying herself, and today MacIain's wife wears a hood under her brow.

I found no locked book in the cottage ruin, and I have chosen to believe it was a bard's house rather than *know* it was. But there was a bardic community hereabouts, set apart from the main Glencoe community, and surely such bards would feed off the mountains and wildest nature? Surely, too, they would pronounce on the Massacre of 1692? It is hardly stretching credibility to suggest that among the bards of Glencoe there was one old one so attuned to her surroundings that she was wise before the event.

So when I rise with the pipit (no larks here) and thrust my bed aside and stand outside the door and read the morning mood of the Sisters while the glen is still quiet and untrammelled by tourism and traffic, I am looking again for a closer bond with the mountains. I am looking for it in the ruins of that earlier era when a rising bard might stand before the threshold and see in the Three Sisters not a picture-postcard cliché-caricature of the glen but the toecaps of a three-footed god whose unseen limbs and torso are crowned by the summit of all Glencoe, all Argyll, Bidean nam Bian.

All the bardic ingredients are in place: Ossian's Cave is a leering eye high on Aonach Dubh, and no Celtic bard could ask for a more fitting overseer than Ossian; the Bodach and the Cailleach (the stuff of many a Gaelic legend in many a landscape) leer back from Glencoe's northern flank; the wild swans *do* linger on Loch Achtriochtan and their flights have thrown many a shadow across the old cottage walls, and doubtless its roof when it had one; and everywhere is the stain and the treacherous stench of the Massacre, still not washed clean, still the most misrepresented episode in all the inglorious repertoire of the Highlands' self-inflicted wounds. Nowhere broods on its own shed blood quite so savagely and to so little effect as the Glencoe landscape. We resurrect it and lie about it because the look of the landscape encourages our prejudice and our preference for an emotional binge over the cold scrutiny of fact:

Glencoe's cheerless Landseercape
was all Victoriana could wish,
grayly cramping
enlightenment's style.
One misty myth
– 'Glen of Weeping' –
was weaned on rain
and clansman's blood
(our most prolific
Highland clichés).
Macdonalds were slain.

Campbells were slandered forever.
Truth was massacred.

So I have crossed the river to look on the cottage from below. If I walk west, I set it against the seepage of light which lets a gray-pink flush brush the sky above the far watershed where the Coe rises. If I walk east, towards the light, I see that the cottage stands on the last shelf of higher ground before the glen flattens and widens out to embrace Loch Achtriochtan. I see too that its survival is due, as much as anything, to the fact that it stands on the wrong side of the river to be conveniently dismantled and its stones used to build the later farm. The same is true of a rag-and-tatter-walled enclosure nearby, following the coughs and hiccups of the ground all the way back to the bottom of the mountains. By implication, the track which serviced that settlement, however long deserted it may be, was on the other side of the river from both the modern road and the military road. You find causeway-like bits of it creeping along under the buttresses. From where I stand, looking up at the ruin, looking east to where the glen rises to its watershed and the mountains lean closest at the throat of the pass, there is a sudden and brief inkling of the glen that was, for it was a cul-de-sac. But however you plough your energies and your imagination into the exercise, you cannot reconvene the elements of a lost landscape. The headlights of a truck cross the watershed, a white lance in the imaginative endeavour of the moment, and the late twentieth century gatecrashes its way remorselessly down the glen with a sooty-blue roar. It is six a.m., and from now on, the glen will only grow noisier, the glen of the cul-de-sac centuries quite beyond reach until the owl hours resume.

I often wonder about that cottage, not least because as one who makes a living writing about and among wild places, I can think of few better jobs than being Glencoe's writer-in-residence three or four hundred years ago. But there is a more significant reason. The fact of its survival means, to me at least, that the thread of continuity which links our heyday to the bards' heyday is not utterly broken. It is frail and worn down to its last skinny strand, but it serves, every time I go in at its fallen slate lintel, to make me question why we have allowed so much of the bloom of the true glen to wither. Glencoe should be a wooded place, but sheep have nibbled away that cloak of nature. Worse, they still do. Glencoe should be lived in, worked in a small way. Instead it is as denuded of a native population as it is of trees. Glencoe should be a vigorous wildlife reservoir. Instead it is impoverished. Glencoe should be cherished for its mountain landscape. Instead it is exploited for it. The National Trust for Scotland's management is led not by the demands of thoughtful conservation but by the demands of tourism. They have not only contravened the very explicit wisdom of their mountain benefactor, Percy Unna (whose energies brought the glen into Trust ownership in the 1930s), but they contravene the very spirit of the place.

Finally, Glencoe should be a cul-de-sac. It is not: it has become a thoroughfare. We have learned much about the worth of landscape since the road was inflicted on it sixty years ago. We could make no grander gesture in recognition of that learning than to realign the road along its natural old course from Kingshouse to Kinlochleven. In the glen itself, a small road need travel no further east than Achtriochtan. Tourism does not need access. Let it walk.

Removing the road and restoring the glen, building the new road, creating a workable agriculture, re-creating a native woodland and managing it for wildlife, breathing back life here, would both render one of our most distinguished and characteristically Scottish landscapes a great service, and also establish a ground-breaking precedent of treating conservation as a major source of sustainable Highland employment.

Conservation is the wrong word. Aldo Leopold wrote in *A Sand County Almanac*:

> The practices we now call conservation are, to a large extent, local alleviations of biotic pain. They are necessary, but they must not be confused with cures.

I have crossed back to the cottage side of the river and packed my sleeping bag and my prejudices. I have climbed and walked and wandered and wondered and dozed through twenty hours alone in the glen. You cannot do such a thing, thinking as you go, without concluding that it is not conservation Glencoe needs but a cure.

Chapter Nine

THE SUPERSTAR

A GOLDEN EAGLE pulls out from the shadow of the mightiest mountain in the West Highlands and begins to fall all over its sky. First it climbs, fast, wings working as hard as a golden eagle's wings ever work; then the wings fold and that recognisably eagle shape is suddenly a blunt shapeless free-falling missile. The speed of the fall and the transformation of the bird are too fast to pin down. I think: what does that *feel* like? What does it sound like? What does it look like hurtling through the icy late-January air and glaring straight down the open throats of An Teallach? Nature does not deal in grander gestures than this, not in this country.

The flight levels out, is eagle again, then folds and falls again, 1000 feet of spilled air, then the outflung spreadeagle of wings, the upward curve, the hard climb, the wheeling crown of the climb, four sunwise circles, then the bird falls again, over, above and around An Teallach. Just before the fall, the last of the circles is woven through the circling of a second eagle. The faller is the male, trying to impress the circler, who is his mate, and if she is unimpressed by this, she shouldn't be an eagle, or so it looks from where I stand.

Where I stand is a no-man's land of the north-west. It is a wild moor above the Dundonnell road, a unique place for its cinemascopic way of looking at An Teallach. It climbs westward as if to butt on to the mountain, but what it does instead is halt fearfully on a clifftop, a three-mile clifftop which is the sidewall of a long tilting saucer of a corrie, Coir' a Ghuibhsachan. Below your feet is a void split by a river into two lands, one the gray edge of the moor, the other the gray-pink climbing mass of rock heaped up into six named summits and nine named corries: collectively the five miles from Strath na Sealga to south shore of Little Loch Broom we call An Teallach. To south and north lies a glut of mountain realms: Knoydart, Kintail, Applecross, Torridon, Fisherfield, Inverpolly, Assynt. In their midst, and palpably none of them is An Teallach, the Forge, the superstar.

The golden eagle is not exactly An Teallach's bird. He is thirled to a ledge far across Strath Beag, but he invades An Teallach's skies on this gray and blackening January afternoon. To my eye, he is all that moves, barely visible without the glasses at the summit of one more bulleting climb. He rises like a fast lift, one flip (climactic minutia of flight, an exquisite minimalist manoeuvre showing the limitlessness of his wings' flexibility) and he is on his back, folding, falling again, and far below, the land is stamped massively with the 'E'-shaped monstrousness of An Teallach. I rarely envy other lives, but I would have given a lot to sense that eagle moment, that languid stall, that tilting of the mountain world and its skies, that compressing of eagle energies into the new downward direction of the fall, nailing An Teallach to the map.

His mate wheels away north, sliding out of her level circling into a long shallow glide. He bounces off a shelf of air far below her and in the space of perhaps twenty seconds is above her, sharing her northward glide.

The day began a moorland mile or two to the east, gray and blackening, every mountain in every direction fending off encampments of ever thicker storm clouds which promised only snow. The moor climbs a brown mile over three crests to a ridge with a cairn at 1000 feet. It wears the shades of some old and faded hunting plaid, grasses washed-out tawny or burnt orange, lochans pale with the snow-sky or gray with half-thawed ice, old snow patches scruffy with the brown blown fragments of the moor, heather mostly. I thought for a moment of my mother's 'bleak' recoil from such a landscape (it was somewhere near here that her small speech and my small awakening occurred all those years ago), and looked at the apparent lifelessness of the place. But the voice of a raven had punctured the mountain quiet all afternoon, and fox droppings in the grass were moist and latticed with the bones and limbs and shells of the moor's lesser lives – vole, beetle, who knows what else. Then as my eyes worked back across my tracks, back up into the blackest northmost sky, it was to catch sight of the eagles for the first time. I followed their flight and they led me down to the western horizon which suddenly revealed what I knew it would, the open-shouldered, snow-hooded breadths and heights and depths of An Teallach, a vast monochrome.

The sky will claim victory over this day. The mountains are slowly succumbing as the cloud creeps down. The moor shrinks as the wind marshalls new forces in the south-east, throws salvoes of squalls before its advance. The sky is inflating, darkening, lowering, energising, but a finger-in-the-dyke of pale cloudlessness, a contracting aperture, lets a ghost light obliquely down on the tiger-striped mountain. A lochan catches that light, holds it briefly through that midwinter metamorphosis, its gray-and-white dullness of ice and old snow punctured at its heart by a circle of melted water. However far I skirt that lochan, it mimics the shades of the far mountains and lies on the moor before me like a welcome mat.

The hole in the sky closes. The lochan dulls, the mountains dull, the sky darkens. New and weightier squalls force the eyes down from horizons and skies to boulders and underfoot intimacies, a lichen burgeoning like a sponge, one small showpiece in the moor's colossal repertoire of lichens.

The mountains have gone. The cloud has met the moor. The lochan hisses at the impact of sleet on its ice sheath, a sound like spilled water on a hot stove. I bow to the day – to the sky – and my last look back to where An Teallach and the eagles have been reveals no trace either of the mountain or the sky which an eagle might scroll . . .

. . . Midnight, a late scent of the air in Ullapool, the wind gone, the growling sky gone, the starry aftermath of the storm hails the new snow. In my mind's eye, I have returned to the moor. I see the lochan reclaim its ice skin and coldly heal the hole at its heart. I see the moor's sky, high now and glittering. I see two eagles, heads in spines, at rest on a north-facing ledge. I see all of the mountains of An Teallach, Fisherfield and Assynt re-emerge into the born-again night, carefree as badgers.

In the morning, I will go back to the moor and marvel at the show the superstar will have made of it all.

It was my second ascent of An Teallach which convinced me that there was too much mountain to just climb it; my second dice with Lord Berkeley's unchancy seat and his bloody army of pinnacled acolytes which reasoned with me and made sense. A tour of this mountain could take a week and not repeat itself. The man who hauls up here in the mist, pats the summit cairn then skips on to bag a Dearg or a Fannich or two is an oaf. If he tells you he has climbed An Teallach he is being economical with the truth. All he has done is pat the summit cairn. In the process, not only has he not climbed the mountain, he has missed the mountain.

My first ascent missed the mountain, and I got nothing more than the gist of the mountain's upper echelons, which on such a mountain renders the whole exercise a bit pointless. The second ascent was still, windless, warm and clear and the kind of May morning which can convince you that the West Highlands are a fair definition of paradise. The problem is that as you drive towards the mountain along Destitution Road it throws you its widest profile, but to climb it, you start almost underneath the mountain, and although it is impressive enough, you only get less than half of it at any one time. The more I climbed that day, the more I grew besotted with the whole mountain, not with its summits and serrations and ridgey intricacies (and certainly not with the view from the top because there is nothing in that vast all-round panorama which compares to the mountain where you stand, and which you cannot see because you are standing on it), but with the whole stockpiled scope of the mountain. So the day after the aborted crossing of the moor I was back, and the summits stood clear and the sun shone and the west wind was shaping the night's new snow and An Teallach's five-mile horizon was the perfect mountain, and this the perfect approach to it. The snow has touched them lightly so that they look newly painted rather than plastered.

The eagles are over the same northern hill, but in long level flight this time, and at this distance, all they seem is small. An Teallach, though, is a wall limiting the world. Such a wall, such a manifold mountain, demands to be watched. Imagine Ben Lomond stitched on to Bla Bheinn, Bla Bheinn to Stobinian, Stobinian to any Gael Charn anywhere. Imagine a huge kite-shaped embellishment fastened to the crown of all that like an overdone white cockade. Imagine all this arranged so that it walls in two secret

An Teallach stormbound, the moor 'wears the shades of some old and faded hunting plaid . . .'

The wall of Coir' a' Ghiubhsachan, 'a dark scribble of contours writhing away from the base of
An Teallach . . .'

Winter spates charge down one of Coir' a' Ghiubhsachain's glittering repertoire of waterfalls

upper chambers. Imagine such a mountain mass wearing the most seductive of all garbs, in which the ermine of new snow is punctuated darkly by buttresses, slabs, fissures, outcrops and gullies. Is there anything finer to look on anywhere when sun and pastel skies predominate, and a broken circle of similarly clad but deferential mountains rings every compass point? I want to walk the moor to the mountain, a line low and level as a questing eagle's flightpath, aimed at the corrie called Toll an Lochain, where lies the beating heart of An Teallach, three miles in which the mountain will grow before me, widening and towering. I want to be drawn in by the mountain, to peer over the rim of the corrie at its beating heart.

There is no better way to treat An Teallach than this, although I believe that had I not climbed to the summit first, I would not have realised the shortcomings of simply climbing it. The mountain comes so highly recommended by all who have climbed here, but few who have climbed have then watched the mountain grow from the moor and learned just how much there really is to recommend.

There is a trough in the moor. From its shelter, from its lowest heathery depth, every hint of the encircling mountains is removed. I paused out of the wind there, and suddenly my surroundings had an acute smallness which I found oddly disconcerting in the midst of the day's preoccupation with space and grand gesture. If you were to be taken to such a place blindfolded, then have the blindfold removed and be compelled westward up out of the trough so that, having no idea where you were, you saw An Teallach rise before you (and if you survived the experience without succumbing to a peculiar perversion of stage-fright), you would never again take mountains or moorland troughs for granted. I tried it.

I went up, unblindfolded and knowing precisely where I was, and having spent no more than half an hour in the trough. I was still fooled, still taken aback. The mountain emerges again as you near the crest. But it emerges from the wings – both wings at once – and reveals its centre-stage last. That initial resighting of the ends of An Teallach recalled in my mind Gavin Maxwell's description of seeing the fin and tail of a basking shark for the first time:

> At first it was no more than a ripple with a dark centre. The centre became a small triangle . . . The triangle grew until I was looking at a huge fin, a yard high and as long at the base. . . A few seconds later the notched tip of a second fin appeared some twenty feet astern of the first . . . It was some seconds before my brain would acknowledge that these two fins must belong to the same creature. The impact of this realisation was tremendous and indescribable: a muddle of excitement in which fear and a sort of exultation were uppermost, as though this were a moment for which I had unconsciously waited for a long time.

So An Teallach broke the surface of the moor before my barely believing eyes, and my first thought was that I was going the wrong way and the two extremities to left and right, south and north, could not possibly belong to the same mountain. But crossing the trough, and my brief respite inside it, had brought me much nearer to the mountain than I had realised, and I saw the whole overawing mass of it again, as though for the first time, rather than (perhaps) the fiftieth.

Climbing the mountain is not like this. Climbing it, you appreciate it as a climber, for what it has to offer that may be climbed or looked at while you climb. Your attention is split: half to the climbing, half to that portion of the mountain which is visible. On An Teallach, the exercise is never less than memorable, but it is not as good as this. Here the travelling makes no demands and the day can drool on the whole mountain, or at least the whole of the east-facing mountain, which is actually only half of it. (For the other half, try shinning up a little two-and-a-half-thousand-footer a couple of miles to the north-west of An Teallach called Sàil Mhór, preferably at sunset: you won't regret it.) Then a punctured fragment of cumulus crosses the sun and pushes a spotlight of intense light round the snow-and-black-rock walls of Toll an Lochain, prodding into its every crevice, striking glints as it passes, a dragnet of diamonds. Had you been climbing there, you might briefly have warmed to its touch as you sought out hand and foothold. From the moorland ridge you see it switch on, see its whole exploration, see it cross the terraces of Glas Meall Liath, see it snuff out in the midst of an airy crossing of Glas Tholl, which is Toll an Lochain's loch-less twin.

The moor becomes mountain where a curious little concave valley dips and climbs up slabby rock slopes to what you have thought for the past hour is the precursor of Toll an Lochain. The mountain has led you to believe that you can step from moorland on to the skirts of the corrie. It is a deception, a half-truth, for to do so you would have to step over a cliff. You have reached the wall of Coir 'a' Ghiubhsachain, a dark scribble of contours writhing away from the base of An Teallach's mighty 'E' like a badly done curlicue. It is here, on a terrace a little below the rim of the cliff, and just below eye-level with Loch Toll an Lochain (a Gaelic perversity meaning the Loch of the Hole of the Lochan which loses a lot in the literal translation) that you win the highest prize that the West Highland landscape-stalker knows, which is as much of the presence of An Teallach as any one viewpoint allows. To go closer means to lose all but the inside of half of the mountain, for to go closer means to go down, then up, and by the time you start upping, you are under the mountain again, and craning to see it. The clifftop, the wall of Coir 'a' Ghiubhsachan, is a rampart, nature's outer defence on the mountain. If you sit here and watch An Teallach for long enough, you will learn much about the mountain and its architecture, for as the light lowers and swings away, dipping to the south-west, the mountain chameleons subtly. The flanks and protruding shoulders grow yellow, while the headwall of the Toll pulls down an unfathomable shadow like a blind.

All day, my eye has returned again and again to the kite shape fixed to the mountain's central skyline, its shape dictated by two summit ridges and two intersecting gullies directly below them. It fascinates as it grows, as its detail emerges, a kite of rock flown by the hot wind of volcanic upheaval which foundered on a mountain top. Or a designer's afterthought, a showy diamond accessory, a coronet fit to grace the forehead of a superstar?

Or perhaps it is an architect's signature, like a Mackintosh rose or an 'exaggerated corbel', for Mackintosh wrote 100 years ago in a famous lecture:

> This is a subject dear to my heart and entwined among my inmost thoughts and affections . . . the architecture of our own country, just as much Scotch as we are ourselves — as indigenous to our country as our wild flowers, our family names, our customs or our political constitution . . . In the castles of the fifteenth century . . . every feature was useful. In the sixteenth century also, however exaggerated some of the corbels and other features might be, they are still distinguished . . . by their genuineness and utility . . . Since then we have had no such thing as a national style . . .

Mackintosh, had he dwelt on such a rock wall from such a viewpoint as mine would have painted it with his faultless architect's eye, drawing on its great verticals, formalising its curves and its strata, pouring it all into the same melting point from which emerged his re-defining of our national style. Look at An Teallach's summit kite. Look at his painting of the rock wall called Le Fort Maillert in Glasgow School of Art. See the same kite shape in the same place, the summit of the rock wall, and its trailing tail of rock fissures, a central cohesive component in the structure of the composition. In an architect with such an eye for landscape, it is no accident. He could have been a supreme painter of the Scottish mountain landscape.

What is 'best' in any architectural style will always be the most subjective of controversies, but it is arguable at least, from a podium on a cliff-edge of Coir 'a' Ghiubhsachain, that in terms of the Scottish school of mountain architecture, here before you is its finest hour, topped off by its outrageous but compositionally crucial kite.

I have been watching the mountain for more than an hour now. Occasionally my eyes drag away from Toll an Lochain and *that* skyline to the outer reaches of the mountain. The sun has slipped low over Sail Liath, and no longer glares off the still surface of Lochan na Bradhan which lies on the watershed. That means I can look the watershed in the face again, and re-address a niggling something-or-other which first occurred to me before the sun started dazzling the lochan. The broad beam of this corner of the mountain has all the characteristics of a classic Highland watershed except one. On its northern side, it sheds no water. By rights it should spill a burn from the lochan down into Coir' a' Ghiubhsachain, feeding the river which charges down through the corrie out of Toll an Lochain. They should meet somewhere about the river's elbow-bend lurch to the north. I could find nothing. I checked the large-scale map. Nothing. The lochan feeds southwards, but nowhere does its shoulder feed northwards. I'm sure it happens elsewhere, but I couldn't remember ever seeing such a thing before.

PREVIOUS PAGE: An Teallach, the superstar, the perfect approach to the perfect mountain

I mention it because of the stag. He must have been in my sightline for as long as I had sat on the clifftop, but my preoccupation with the mountain had closed my mind to what was going on below. What was going on was that a stag was eating its way up to the watershed from the corrie floor and was about to pass directly beneath where I sat, perhaps 100 feet below me. He moved badly. He was slow and alone, and in a red deer stag at the end of the winter, these are not good omens. He was also climbing out of the shelter of the corrie, away from the feeding and cover of the woodland at its north end, and although he paused often to browse, there was barely a bite from top to bottom of the pass he climbed. Then there was the climb itself. It was ferociously steep and would have pressed a fit beast hard. And it was utterly dry.

In the glasses I could see that both his antlers were broken. The old head and neck were thick and gray, but the body was all too thin. The legs, especially the hind legs, were simply not up to the task he had set them. He stopped again and just stood, unalert. It is a hard land for a red deer in the best of seasons, but this is the worst of seasons, and he had chosen to climb the worst of mountain walls, the one with no water, and next to no grass amid its wind-polished rocks. Had our paths crossed in his autumn prime, he would have looked magnificent on that slope. Monarch of the Glen may be a cliché, but with the best of stags in the finest of glens, it can trip off the tongue aptly enough. But monarchs can be overthrown: the mountain was done with this stag, and the stag done with the mountain. A fit stag in such a landscape looks invincible. The stag below me simply looked small.

I paused often on my way back across the moor to look back at the mountain, to wonder about the stag as withered as a dried-out watershed.

The mountain looks greatest at its greatest distance, a softly unlit iceberg aglow with snowlight, settling low in the dark brown sea of the moor. The moor's every edge is attended by such icebergs, Fisherfield, the Fannichs, the Deargs across the Dirrie More . . . all of them distant and pale, all of them head-turners, all of them basking in the reflected glory of the superstar, none of them capable of holding a candle to it. But of all the moors and wild places I have trekked to keep the company of mountains, there is one more moor I hold closer. It is the one I crossed to meet the Soloist, and came away a gladder and a wiser man.

'To come on Suilven for the first time, unsuspecting, is to have your ideas and imagery of the Highlands redefined'

Chapter Ten

THE SOLOIST

THE LAND OF Inverpolly and Assynt lies aslant. Its every gesture urges north-west. At its heart, three mountains individual as pyramids swim north-west against thick ripples of contours. You do not get the feeling of being 'among' mountains here, at least not in the sense of Torridon or Glencoe or the Cairngorms. Yet in another sense, the whole landscape, even the low-lying spaces between the summits, is shrunken mountain. And while the mountains stand apart on miles-wide plinths of space, alone as milestones, you cannot step beyond the force-field of a mountain realm.

The centrepiece of all this is not so much a mountain (at 2400 feet there are any number of higher bland upland summits) as a rock. *The* Rock. The best single Rock in all Scotland, the Soloist, Suilven; the most shocking consummation of that old wedding of Lewissian gneiss and Torridonian sandstone which spawned a tribe of grizzled hybrids characteristically distinctive enough to become their own geological species. You see it first in Applecross. You lose the sense of it by the time you reach the north coast. Suilven is its archetype. To come on Suilven for the first time, unsuspecting, unwarned, even after Torridon, even after An Teallach, is to have your ideas and imagery of the Highlands redefined. It is no place for the land-squeamish. Suilven offers you no gradual evolution, no warnings, no compromises. I love it for that. What you see is what you get, and you get it all at once. Except . . .

. . . I have stolen a day from May and transplanted it into February. The sun is low and cold in mid-morning, the north-facing flanks and corries of Cul Mor across the Cam Loch shadowed and snowed and dark. The shoreline path is hard and frosted. Suilven is there, a far skyline shape, implausible as always, foreshortened from here but unquestionably itself – blunt and round pachyderm forehead, hacked dinosaur spine, tail of . . . tail of nothing that springs to mind, a pointed 2000-foot jab into the Sutherland air.

The day has a simple mission. It is to unearth the other unseen (by me at least) Suilven, that Suilven which, if the map is to be believed, will climb from the high moor as a single pinnacle concealing all the mountain's familiar shape – no long ridge, no barging forehead. I want to stand on a fixed point high on the moorland edge and photograph what I hope will be a monumental landscape fluke, a majestic deception. As I walk the morning lochshore and feel the day slowly warm to the occasion, I ask myself why. Why put in a rough fourteen-mile day not to climb a mountain but merely to look at it, not to touch it but to keep it purposefully at arms' length, not to present the true character of the mountain but a corruption of it? The answers I contrive tread dangerous ground, for they have to do with that throwback notion which treats mountains – or certain mountains at least – as rather more than just upthrusts in a landscape. That aloof and solitary rearing aspect of Suilven which invites you to consider it not as a mountain but as a rock suggests to me immediately a kind of sanctity-in-landscape. It is an ancient response in mankind to regard singular landscape features with a primitive reverence. Mostly we have lost the knack or the urge or the instinct, but you can still stand on Dunadd, hilltop capital of Dalriadan kings 1500 years ago, and feel subjected to an unnameable power. There, the essence is concentrated into the summit rocks among tangible evidence, an inscription, a footprint, a boar, all carved or cut into the rock, the magnetism of an otherwise unprepossessing hill. The power of Ayers Rock to move men is also ancient and documented, and still contrives to overcome sentimental and commercial infiltrations. The essence there is also a concentration – of light, the sunset-reddening of the rock. Is it coincidence, *wholly*, that two men whose work I have admired – Michael Andrews and David Craig – have pursued it and caught it?

So, in the pursuit of the essence of The Rock, Suilven, I am seeking out that concentration of all its energies, the single-malt distillation of all my familiarities into a single, slim Matterhorn thrust. Surely something will rub off if the thing works, if the map hasn't lied, if the day holds good?

On the shore of the Cam Loch, I pause to examine a waist-high rock. I know it is a rock only by scraping a portion of its surface clear, for it is aswarm with invading hordes of moss and lichen, such a fertility in a land of stone! It is good for the eye and the landscape watcher to have his far-mountain preoccupations tripped up by small glories about his feet.

Cul Mor across the loch is massive and multi-form, constantly reshaping. It is a mountain you can circumnavigate and lose your every point of reference mile after mile. Suilven also changes, but from here all it does is telescope closed, and never becomes anything unrecognisably Suilven . . . a thin wedge, an upturned keel.

Cul Mor reveals an old man, a Bodach, a rock pinnacle on a skyline for all the world like a seated figure. I invest him with a pipe and envy him his permanence, for surely his sightline rests on Suilven. If you are to be immortalised for a few thousand million years as a pillar of stone, you may as well be Torridonian sandstone atop Lewissian gneiss and frozen into perpetual contemplation of Suilven. The map declines to name him, but two wilderness miles north-west from the cliff at his feet, the map bears the unlikely word, 'shieling', so now I know where he lived.

My idle fancy done, I look again at that word on the map, trying to translate it into a human existence. The shieling stands, or at least stood, above a tiny, supremely sheltered bay on Loch Sionascaig, miles from any discernible small centre of population, or even from a discernible track which leads to one. Who would seek out such a thing for the summer pasturing of beasts in such a place? You shake your head over the possibility, and marvel at the tenacity with which folk once clung to such a land for a living, rage at the forces which drove them out. Then you trace a finger back along the same grid line a couple of squares and find, on another shore of the same loch, 'Boat Bay', and a small track linking it with the modern road to Lochinver. So did the shieling folk go in that way, by boat? The Bodach would know. He would know because for all the joys of his stone-eyed watch, he would also have presided over the draining of human lifeblood from the land at his feet, that blood of which the shieling's ruin was a shed droplet. He would learn with some satisfaction, though, that in Assynt of all places, this same land, in 1992, a war of bloodless words was waged which poured crofting blood back into the land, and no drop was shed. He will learn in his own definition of time whether that small momentousness was a turning tide or just a ripple on an old, still pool.

My path inclines away from the Cam Loch. I turn my back on the old man, Suilven slinks behind the rising ground, and in the warm noon of this unlikeliest February day, I head for the high moors of Assynt in shirt sleeves. Red deer hinds and calves pause in their meagre feeding to pose or panic, blessing the day too, although they will have the night to thole, fourteen hours of freezing darkness.

Leaving the path is guess-work, for now the only mountain reference point is the long wall of Canisp. I turn blindly into the beautiful snow-patched winter moor, and my greeting is from a golden plover. He wears his uninspiring winter coat, as wan an echo of his gold and black breeding plumage as the winter moor's poor resemblance to its spring and summer vigour. He calls once, a falling two-syllable note for which the word 'plaintive' might have been invented. I follow his flight in the glasses, a sweep which encompasses the entire length of Cul Mor. He is early and alone. I look at the terrain where his winter flight has stalled. The moor rises ahead in endless folds. Somewhere beyond one of them is a glimpse of Suilven's Matterhorn summit, I hope. Canisp is all the world there is to the north, massively flanking a long glen. Cul Mor is south of my left shoulder, irrelevant for the moment. Over my right shoulder is another stunningly sculpted set piece of the Sutherland landscape, Quinag, a snow-white cliff where waves of brown moor hills break.

A rock cuts the moorland skyline, pointed and ridged almost vertically, right up the middle. I race up a fifty-foot moorland bank: Suilven – the top two hundred feet perhaps. Another quarter of a moorland mile takes me under the next rise, and the mountain is obliterated again. I climb again, and a bit more is bared, then lost to one more rise in the moor. There are a dozen such infuriating rises until a marked freshening of the wind announces a cliff edge, and I step on to the hard-floored small plateau of Meall na Braclaich and the moor has no defences left. The name means the Hill of the Fox Cairn or the Hill of the Badger Sett, and more likely fox than badger at

1200 feet, but it is a curiosity of the Gaelic language which lumps them both together in a crude definition of vermin, and the *broclair* was the keeper, the destroyer of vermin. Meall na Braclaich, or Broclach, then, is a foxy kind of place, with its broken, tumbledown cliff, but it deserves a better name, for it contemplates the Matterhorn.

I had imagined what Suilven might look like from here, but not this. The raw rock of Sutherland's ground floor sculpts itself up through that yellowing winter light, up into a single slim and stupendous spire. A wedge of the same rock trails away north from the spire's base the way a plover feigns a broken wing. All around lies the lower chaos of Sutherland, smoothed foundations of that ancient and shrunken mountain from which Suilven leans up, named and nameless rock (shores, plateaux, buttresses, small cliffs), lochs and lochans and rivers and burns and less-than-burns. Every sense of that mountain Norman MacCaig called 'my masterpiece of masterpieces' is lost. Instead there is only this snow-streaked monolith standing alone on the moor's great stillness.

A ridge splits the spire from pinnacle to plinth like a badly fashioned seam, so that the sun catches only one half of the mountain. The other shadowed half is where the snow lingers. I watch the lowering, yellowing light deepen through a long and mesmerising afternoon hour. I have come here to distil a mountain and to revere it. But instead, I gawp and so does my camera. It feels uncomfortable, like a camcorder in a cathedral. Something inside rebukes such conduct, but I impress on myself too the need to get it down, overdose on it, the distillation can come later. If I come back, perhaps the revering can start then? Slowly the mood calms and mountain and I watch each other for an hour more of my life, a blink of the mountain's eternity.

A thought lodges. How many people who think they know Suilven have seen this? Few for sure, very few. This moorland nowhere of the fox-badger is the only place where it works. Half a mile to the south, the south flank of the mountain unfolds again and the blunt elephant skull (which is the Suilven of Lochinver) thrusts out an ear. In the glen to the north it's the same. Only this trackless, plover-haunted moor accommodates the secret Suilven, and only a Matterhorn-hunter or a fox-exterminator has a purpose in being here. The urge on me now is to stay and stay, to watch the yellow drain from the mountain leaving it smouldery gray, to watch the gray drain from the mountain leaving it black against eggshell off-white skies. But it is three-thirty p.m. and it will be dark by six and there are seven rough miles to go.

I go reluctantly. This hasn't gone deep enough. This was the quest to find my own Dunadd, to isolate my Ayers Rock and kindle sacred fires in it, to distil Suilven, The Rock, down to a single pure strand, a totem. The Rock exceeded all my expectations, the spectacle haunting, uncanny. But sacred? I wave at my Matterhorn and begin to reel in the moor again, dropping down its folds, pausing above each one to look back at the diminishing mountain. I want nothing else in my mind, but Sutherland will have

PREVIOUS PAGE: *Suilven as Matterhorn: 'How many people who think they know Suilven have seen this?'*

none of that. The sun teeters on the summit silhouette of Cul Mor, and as I begin the descent to the lochshore, it dips behind. So begins a long dusk of awesome beauty, the sorcery of the sun working behind Cul Mor's back. The mountain re-emerges from its own silhouette, for now the unlit northern faces are illuminated by their own snow, a soft-focus mountain with hard edges.

Loch whitens, shores blacken. The sky above Cul Mor moves through yellow to orange, and lights an orange flarepath down a dipped shoulder of the mountain to flood a small bay, a vivid spillage of colour.

From the lochshore now, Suilven has reassumed its nonchalant hunch. The yellow has gone and the restored familiarity of its profile grows gray and grayer, as though it was ageing before my eyes. The moon has been in the sky all afternoon. Now it takes over to light the last black mile along the loch. Hinds cluster nearby, waiting for me to pass, leaving their path clear to the lochside. There are many tracks in the shoreline sand. I think of them an hour from now, drinking in the moonlight, the moon fingering among the old snows of Cul Mor, Suilven growing youthful again in its light.

One last pause restores the old perspectives. Cul Mor is hidden and Suilven stands alone and far off, gray and vague as a shroud draped over a rock, yet such a shapelessness is so arranged that its only possible name is Suilven.

And what of the day's quest? What of the Dunadd in my mind, the Ayers Rock afire, a distillation of Suilven, The Rock, to hold sacred and revere? I have relived that day many times in my mind, and if I have learned one thing from it, it is that you cannot invent a sacred rock, no matter how great its age or splendour. There is no such thing as a sacred rock. There is only rock, and whether it is a thousand million years old or three thousand million hardly matters, except to those who count the years of rock for a living. Great age does not impart sanctity on a rock, nor does an aesthetically striking profile. There is nothing particularly impressive in the profiles of Dunadd or Ayers Rock. A society or a community or a solitary wandering man can look to a certain mountain and derive comfort (or discomfort for that matter) from its presence, and so elevate the mountain's status in his mind. Because of where it stands in relation to where it is seen from, it may be that its way of harnessing sunrise or sunset or snow or storm has prompted people to revere it, even place their Gods there, or perhaps to look to the mountain as nothing more than a kind of barometer. But, unless you believe in the story of Mt Sinai, any sense of sanctity has been conferred by man, and invariably it is the fruit of long tradition. You take the mountain as you find it and you respond to it. You do not take the mountain and try and turn it into something else. I should have known that, for I have been moved by rock before, when I have trodden ancient paths and taken the rock as I found it. But I was asking too much of the Suilven trek. It was a good thing to do, and the secret corner of the mountain was worth watching. I should have left it at that. The claim I was trying to stake there was a futile one. My 2000-foot Matterhorn simply failed to distil anything of the sense of Suilven, or rather I failed to distil anything from it.

*'A rock cuts the moorland skyline, pointed and ridged almost vertically, right up the middle –
Suilven . . .'*

'So begins a long dusk of awesome beauty, the sorcery of the sun working behind Cul Mor's back . . .'

'Suilven, The Rock . . . it distils best at its grayest. I should have known that. I know it now'

But when I replay that trek in my mind now, I remember two mountains: the Suilven-Matterhorn I stalked across the high moor like a prime stag, and the last sighting of all, Suilven as a distant rock draped in a gray shroud. It is that second mountain I revere, the familiar rendered down in the almost-darkness to nothing more than a hint of a shape, a thing of little more substance than shadows, but still possessing substance enough to be unquestionably the Suilven I know and love, the mountain kernel, the perfect, the ultimate distillation. The yellow light on the afternoon Matterhorn may have approximated to the sunset-fire of Ayers Rock. The spire's summit may have crudely recalled the summit rocks of Dunadd. But if you take the mountain as you find it, Suilven, *The* Rock, is all summit, summit of that shrunken mountain land it inhabits, and it is gray. It distils best at its grayest. I should have known that. I know it now.

Chapter Eleven

AMONG ISLANDS

I HAD NEVER seen such a mountain. It was a blue-shadowed stockpile of broken pyramids and it stood forward from a hot mountain haze. And above all the pyramidal mass there rose a single final pyramid, climbing to a perfect pencil-point summit, the still centre it seemed, of a whirling dervish of ridges. It was on one of those ridges I stood, and for someone who hitherto had climbed only among the Angus Glens and the Cairngorms, I contemplated my surroundings with more or less equal portions of fear, disbelief, awe, and joy. My companion's malicious sense of humour insisted on quoting from a little guidebook whose writer delighted in a gently cynical line of understatement: he now warned that 'the only difficulty is a tricky little *mauvais pas*'.

A *what*?

My school French was still fresh enough in my mind then to diagnose 'bad step'. That in turn conjured in my mind – not from experience but from my mountain-crowded bookshelves – Poucher-esque images of *The* Bad Step in the Skye Cuillin, and that was enough to quicken the pulse unhealthily. What was it about island mountains which invented such a perversity of obstacles to bestrew the path of a good day out?

Another thing: why were the mountains so skinny? Where were the boulevard-broad mountain shoulders? This ridge where I now stood would disgrace a single-track pavement and it writhed like an old pine branch. Where were the boulderfields, the ptarmigan couches, the piles and piles of skies? And what was that light? That luminescent air that charged even a heat haze with a shimmering vitality? Come to think of it, where were the miles and miles of other mountains and hills and lesser upthrusts crumpling away to the edge of the mountain world?

It had all begun innocuously enough – doesn't it always – a plausible glen called Sannox, a steep plod up Suidhe Fhearghas, cloud on the tops but the day promising the kind of sun which would burn all that away. A common gull preening on a boulder at 2000 feet suggested the island nature of the place, and it watched as we passed and followed us for half a ridgey mile. I chose to interpret it as a good omen. Then I saw the mountain. It was the pivot, not just of the day but of all Arran. It stood at the centre of everything, and by its exquisite strength and the Catherine-wheel curves of its ridges it seemed to suspend the whole island up out of the sea, an illusion which the haze only heightened. If you watched it long enough you could imagine it beginning to revolve and play like a slow merry-go-round. Its name was Cir Mhor, and I had never stared perfection in the face before, never been confronted by the power of the aesthetics of a beautiful mountain.

It was there, too, besotted by spectacle, that I encountered for the first time a conflict which has grown in me ever since, so that now it is at the very heart of all my wanderings among mountains. It is the conflict between the self-indulgence of the mountaineer and the dignity of the mountain. Before Cir Mhor, I was on the side of the mountaineer; I am now utterly converted to the cause of the mountain. But that day on Cir Mhor, I heard the mountain's silent submission for the first time, and for a year or two thereafter, I trod a path of equipoise as narrow and treacherous as the A'Chir (Cir Mhor's most outrageous spur). But you cannot balance the needs of man against the needs of the mountain: when man turns a piece of mountain to his own uses, thereby belittling the mountain, he cannot then offer the mountain a piece of himself. The two are at loggerheads and will be until man is willing again, as he once was, to walk softly among mountains and leave no trace of his passing. So I came down off my ridge of neutrality and uncertainty, determined to champion the mountain against my own kind. Cir Mhor sowed a seed in me which rooted and grew, an evergreen truth. It is that the beautiful mountain matters. It is the first and last refuge of wildest nature, and it matters most, not because of what we can get out of it, but for itself.

So I stood on the ridge between Ceum na Caillich and Caisteal Abhail, and the mountaineer in me wanted nothing more than to skip over and round the curving, crusty ridges to the pyramid mountain, to put my own small silhouette on top of the pencil point. But suddenly I had for company an embryonic mountain philosopher inhabiting the same body, albeit one who still slaked his thirst with Creamola Foam rather than the pure, unsullied granite-chilled sources of mountain water.

With Cir Mhor I began to look at certain mountains the way others contemplate cathedrals. You can experience in a cathedral something which goes beyond mere religion: it is that there was a time when our own species was so passionately committed to an ideal that they unearthed their highest endeavours of daring and creativity and aesthetic wholeness to acknowledge the ideal. In the process, fusionless louts grew into master craftsmen and walked anonymously away and dignified the landscape of our towns. In Cir Mhor, I saw, a little to the south-west of Suidhe Fhearghas, my first cathedral of nature and its spires were almost at eye level. In twenty years the image has not faded and the philosopher in me has learned to do without the froth and drink from pure springs . . .

. . . So how *mauvais* was the *pas?* I could see the ridge at my feet. I could see the ridge a bit more than a yard away. I could see no ridge in between, only a thrusting boulder with a ledge. The boulder apart, I could see no piece of mountainside which

Cir Mhor sowed a seed in me, an evergreen truth. It is that the beautiful mountain matters

Towards the Witch's Step, one of Arran's delectable fretwork ridges

bore any physical relationship to the sudden absence of ridge. The scale of the headlong descent which would reward a missed footing looked incalculable then, but scanning the map now suggests about 1500 feet without bouncing, down into Coire nan Ceum.

Ah, Ceum; that word jogs the mountaineer's memory out of his cathedral worship. It is Gaelic's equivalent of *pas*, simply 'step'. In an Arran context it refers to Ceum na Caillich, translated by all who have trembled there as 'The Witch's Step'. The *mauvais pas* then is not the Ceum itself (that is a gouge from ridge to glen floor you can see for miles, and inflicted by the Devil's tail or the Witch's broomstick in flight from some nefarious expedition or other). It's a witchy afterthought to ensnare those who have not been overcome by the Ceum. The Ceum is a bit of the ridge which is missing; the *pas* is a bit of the path which is missing. The Ceum entails climbing down from the ridge into the jaws of the Devil's rearrangement of the mountainside, then climbing up out again; the *pas* is just a couple of heart-in-the-mouth steps, but what is *mauvais* about it is that it treads so close on the heels of the Ceum and calls for calm and caution and an unexcited demeanour so soon after the exhilarating flirtation with the Caillich. That and the chilling invitation from the far beckoning floor of the corrie, which may have something to do with the witch-whispers in your ear.

For me, the Ceum, and the *pas*, my inexperience in such a mountain realm, the unhinging isolation of the mountain group with its absence of reference points and sea hazes, all that would have been turmoil enough. But before all that, I had framed a blue pyramid in the foreground boulders of the ridge, and built cathedrals in my mind while a cup of Creamola Foam reverberated inside me. It was all an uncanny burden for a young mountaineer making his debut among islands. It would also prove to be far from unique, for mountains among islands are free with such chains of events, piling sensations like pyramids on an Arran ridge.

I remember nothing of Caisteal Abhail, although we lunched there and admired the growing proximity of Cir Mhor and I let my eye wander over newly revealed ridges. I think it was there that I grew most uncomfortably aware of the absence of a great mass of neighbouring mountains, which is the predominant presence of Highland mountains. There was a summit of squarish slabby battlements, and ridges which fell away hazily down to the island which fell away hazily to the sea. The Peak of the Castles is a cornerpost of the Arran mountains whose nearest mountain kin are on Jura and Mull. To sit here on such a day of warm, ocean-going curtains and their sluggish winds is to know what a gull does for a living. You feel as if you could step off and alight carelessly on Kintyre.

I grew impatient for the blue pyramid, but like all pyramids, it grows blunt and softens its hard edges, and betrays the method of its construction the closer you get. I don't know what I expected, and what there was looked shapely and upstanding enough, but it was not a pyramid. A tinge of disappointment touched my vision of this mountain from afar.

The summit was tiny, and cramped with two people. I stood on it and waved, remembering my ambition of hours before to put my own silhouette on the pencil point of the pyramid. My companion held a hearty sandwich in both hands and was about to bring his jaws to bear on it when he looked up at me and caught me in the act of waving. With the sandwich held two inches from his mouth, he asked 'What are you doing?'

'I'm waving to myself three hours ago on the Witch's Step,' I said.

He raised one eyebrow, and at the same moment thrust the sandwich irredeemably forwards, and with an infinitely less perceptible movement sadly shook his head. He lived here, you see, and he could race up these ridges in his spare time or play golf, and it didn't really matter which. I enjoy golf too, but mostly I play it on courses which have a view of the mountains, and mostly when I do, I am aware that I would rather be two clubs' length from a mountain burn.

The haze which had swithered about the morning swithered through the afternoon too, so the only sense of where I was hung on the threads of flimsy looking ridges which dipped and wandered off into wide blue yonders like drunks. A' Chir is the drunkest of these, a skinny, troublesome little thing, especially in a west wind, where every other *pas* is a bit *mauvais*. If you do not have *la tête solide*, find another way. Cir, or A' Chir for that matter, derives prosaically from comb, or perhaps the crest of a cockerel which is at least mildly more appropriate as both have something to crow about. Another ridge, the bulwark between Coire nam Fuaran of Glen Sannox and the Dearg Chorein of long and lovely Glen Rosa, leapfrogs buoyantly up to the 'back' of Goat Fell, which is the Arran everyone knows because tourism and the National Trust for Scotland traffic-police you that way. Organisations which regard visitor statistics as a yardstick of success should not own mountains, because their definition of success fails the mountain. They acquire the mountain because it is beautiful, then ensure that its rights are trampled underfoot and it grows ugly. It is too easy and too prevalent, this tourist-fodder school of mountain management. It requires no imagination: it takes famous mountains with roadside access, builds them car parks, sacrifices them and calls the process heritage protection. It caters for everything but the true mountain. The true mountain is denied.

That famous 'face' which Goat Fell presents to Brodick Bay is no such thing. It is the mountain's turned back. The true Goat Fell is not an isolationist but one of that small but beautifully formed pack of Arran mountains which whirl on the end of the blue pyramid's skinny, hazy ridges. Something of this, only a germ of it, was already in my mind as I sat on the summit of Cir Mhor, and if *that* was Goat Fell, up there on its ridge-end, above its corrie wall, atop its scalloped seashell-smooth mountain walls, and throwing its own small ridges out into space even while it dangled on the end of Cir Mhor's ridge . . . if *that* was what Goat Fell amounted to, there was something missing and something amiss from what was being peddled to tourism round by Brodick. The seed of a great and elemental doubt was sown. Much later, I would learn that Norman MacCaig, sublime mountain poet, had already written it in two lines:

AMONG MOUNTAINS

There are more reasons for hills
Than being steep and reaching only high

I was still puzzling them out then (I suppose I still am), but some of the other reasons for hills were beginning to dawn on me. Before I had tight-roped my way up to Cir Mhor, I had been as taken in as anyone by tourism's all-pervasive tea-towel Goat Fell. After Cir Mhor I came to think of that mountain profile as one small corner, an outward-facing flank, of an inward-facing network of mountains. Tourism's Goat Fell denies the mountain its true landscape significance, and turns it into something else because it is the highest point of the island, and as bad luck would have it, the handiest.

Does it matter? Yes, it does, and for two reasons. One is that you are offered a two-dimensional watered-down deception when you are urged by the tea-towel trade on to Goat Fell. The result is a smashed-up, ground-down mountain path from Brodick to the summit, the beautiful rendered ugly. The second reason is more complicated, for it has to do with that missing third dimension. There *are* more reasons for hills than being steep and reaching only high, and on the summit of Cir Mhor in the haze and the heat and the blue island air, the mountaineer in me was looking for reasons, and that elusive dimension niggled away at me the way an underground spring niggles at cold granite, and issues up out of the dark and on to the mountain thin as a heather stem. But given time and miles and rain and the prospering waters of other mountains, it gains the fluent certainty of rivers.

We two pyramid dwellers came down from the mountain fulcrum of all Arran at last, sped down what the wee book called 'a shattered whin gully' (whin to me then was what Sassenachs called gorse), a heady species of rough-bottomed chute tending perilously close to the vertical in places. Then we dawdled down Glen Sannox, and I was in the grip of a quiet and introverting euphoria as I reassembled all the day's components and made nonsense of jigsaw-piece thoughts and theories that wouldn't fit. The sun paused on the ridge of Suidhe Fhearghas more or less where the gull had perched eons ago. It split the air of the glen with a single stupendous diagonal – half shadow, half a vivid blue-gray clarity in which Cir Mhor defined itself more sharply than it had done all day and as deceptive from here as Brodick's Goat Fell. And all the way down the glen the missing third dimension was a voice in me, soft and shy and subdued, but stubborn and determined to have its say, and over many years and among many mountains, it has found its tongue. But its first words were here. Sannox was a clue. I was almost beyond its grasp again, almost down at the road and the sea and that other Arran outwith the mountains' sphere. I thought how far *back* Cir Mhor had retreated into the mountains, how deep was that shadowed half of the glen beneath the sun's diagonal. I envisaged that shadow as a wedge, a triangular tunnel, or a long tent wall hung from the ridgepole of Suidhe Fhearghas, the Witch, and the rest.

Sannox is a glacier's scooped spoor, a practically perfect imprint. The ice which fell away and away from the entombed heart of Arran was both glutton and stylist. So little is left of the mountain mass, but shallow corries and mountain walls almost as thin as

132

'Glen Sannox is a glacier's scooped spoor, a practically perfect imprint . . .'

their ridges. A cross-section of Sannox is a huge unbroken curve, but Cir Mhor at its head is all points and angles and hard edges. The contrasting shapes, the shadow and the sun and indefinable island-ness about the landscape . . . these are the raw ingredients from which a young wanderer among mountains who had just stepped down from his first pyramid might first suspect – a hint of an inkling – that the third dimension matters, the *depth* of mountains.

Sannox springs to mind in Sligachan, first thoroughfare of the Skye Cuillin with Marsco an unconvincing stand-in for Cir Mhor. But once, on a late spring afternoon I saw the sun pause on a ridge of Sgurr nan Gillean and throw that old familiar jaw-dropping diagonal into the curve of a deep, deep glen.

Depth among mountains is a multi-faceted dimension. It is something I have sensed best on islands, and in Skye in particular, partly because I know it best, but also because perception of it is unquestionably assisted by an unrivalled quality of light. I once interviewed the late W. A. Poucher, the Bodach of mountain photographers, whose book *The Magic of Skye* in its original large first-edition format is still the best photographic monograph of the Skye landscape for all that many others have tried since. He told me that he would rather work on Skye than anywhere else in the world and advanced the singular reason: 'It's the light.' He also spoke almost reverentially of the Cuillin, called them 'Nature's masterpiece in the Highlands'. He understood the depth of mountains and photographed it wonderfully in black and white (though he never caught it, in my estimation at least, in his later colour work).

It is, in my own contorted and ill-formed definition, a way of looking at mountains which reveals their architecture, their 'insides', the way they were put together. Exploring it (on the good days, which have nothing to do with weather) I sometimes sense an atmosphere of suppressed tension, almost a mountain language in which ancient tongues converse exchanging inconceivable truths. It is this obsession of mine with the mountains' secrets which inclines me to pursue such an obscure aspect of them.

I rarely go to the Cuillin now, for I find myself at odds with what climbing has done to them, ill-at-ease with the technicolour revolution, with the fad for climbing to be seen and heard rather than to see and to hear, with the hordes who bestrew the famous peaks. This is the Goat Fell mentality at work again, for Skye promotes itself shamelessly with its celebrated mountain silhouettes, the Cuillin from Sligachan, the Cuillin from Elgol, the Cuillin from Tarskavaig, from Portree, from Portnalong, from just about anywhere. Yet I still go, because they are so free with their secrets, because their depths are so blatant. So when I go, I try and go quietly and alone and thoughtful, for nowhere is there such a treasury of the secrets of the mountains' third dimension.

If your mountain preferences linger, like mine, around Skye and the Cairngorms, they will not have lingered long without encountering the work of Seton Gordon. He wrote more than twenty books about the Highland landscape and its wildlife and its people, and thousands of newspaper and magazine articles. Two cornerstones from what I believe to be an unsurpassed body of work were *The Cairngorm Hills of Scotland* (1925) and *The Charm of Skye – The Winged Isle* (1929) and both realms infiltrated many more of his books.

He was in his prime during the heyday of the great virtuosos of Scottish rock-climbing, but he was much more of an unclassifiable mountain wanderer, a mountaineer in the broadest possible sense to whom mountain wildlife, especially eagles (which he studied all his life), and mountain people were as much a part of the experience of being among mountains as the mountains themselves. He dwelt often, too, amid the depths of mountains, and although he wrote about many summits he wrote much more about things outwith mere climbing. He too was a pursuer of the mountain secrets rather than a bagger of peaks or a scaler of rock walls.

One expedition he outlined in *The Charm of Skye* so caught my fancy that I decided to emulate it, perhaps sixty years after the event. It was a simple enough plan: start from Glen Brittle, climb to the Bealach a' Gharbh-choire on the Cuillin ridge by way of Coir a' Ghrunnda, then down the Gharbh-choire to Loch Coruisk, climbing down into the dusk and back into the dawn. Why should such a trek appeal to Seton Gordon? He offers a characteristically fey explanation:

> Many writers have praised the beauty of Loch Coruisk, many artists have painted it, but few have seen it beneath the midnight sky. In the silent, windless watches of the night, Loch Coruisk casts a spell that is graven deep in the memory, for by moonlight it has more affinity with the world of dreams and visions than even the ocean at sunset or the Isles lying asleep beneath the pale fingers of the Aurora.

It is a stiff, scrambly climb up to Coir a' Ghrunnda and stiffer by far from there to the bealach, and the Garbh Choire in Seton Gordon's phrase was 'desperately rough' and he was not a man to use a word like 'desperately' lightly. All this to pursue dreams and visions! I love it! He knew that simply by making such a trek, and choosing his time and his season to give him late light and quiet hours, and approaching that steely-gray Cuillin heartland at dusk and in an open-minded spirit . . . he knew that something, some secret of the mountains, some revealed depth, was bound to rub off. It all resembled my own purposes among mountains so closely that I set out on a May day of my own, eager as Columba landing on a Skye shore. I was urged on my way, too, by another good omen. Loch Coruisk is the Loch of the Corrie of Waters; Loch Coir' a Ghrunnda is the Loch of the Corrie of the Earth. Surely there was an elemental nicety about journeying from Earth to Water, by way of Air on the ridge which had the smack of pilgrimage about it. Only Fire was missing, and the Aurora was a bit much to hope for.

I knew Coir' a Ghrunnda of old, for it is my best-loved Cuillin depth. It is their one true high loch, and if you would learn why it is climbers rave and slaver over the virtues of gabbro without actually climbing the Pinnacle Ridge or the Inaccessible Pinnacle, you get every Cuillin ambience you could wish for (apart from the hairy exposure of the

The Cuillin of Skye . . . 'I go because they are so free with their secrets . . .'

skinny ridges) by limpeting up into the corrie. The loch lies at almost 2500 feet, and the only thing clearer than its water is air. It lies in the lap of Sgurr Alasdair, which is no bad place to lie, and it has a sandy beach. It is worth resisting the temptation to swim in it on the kind of relentless days the Cuillin occasionally devise when the rock throws heat back at you and the ridges are full of people with tongues lolling like bloodhound's ears because they haven't brought any water and the Cuillin ridges don't have any. It is a mistake you only make once. Having made it once, I stocked up at the loch, filled a flask, dipped a toe into the coldest water this side of Spitzbergen, and settled for a dip much later in the day and much lower down the mountain.

It would have been a better day for my overnight expedition than the one I chose, but the idea only dawned years later, and as Seton Gordon specified May, I found a May of my own with a space in it and a confident weather forecast, cloud lifting, fine evening, good moon, clear skies. But in addition to a good forecast in the Cuillin you need luck, and mine had run out.

So, at the loch for the second time, and armed with a photocopy of Seton Gordon's pages as I climbed, I sat for an afternoon hour waiting for the summits and the ridge to clear. They never did. My going, I had decided, would have the secondary purpose of comparing my own experience with the maestro's, so that I could assess how much the opportunities he had to taste the Cuillin quietude had dwindled in my own time. For example, he wrote:

> May in the Cuillin is a time of intense silence

and in wildlife terms, which is what he had in mind, it still is. But his May days were uncluttered by the advance guard of the climbing herd's summer-long assault. Sitting on the shore of Loch Coir' a Ghrunnda sipping moodily on hot coffee and eyeing the cloud-draped ridge 400 feet above me, it was the absence of silence which was intense. Between cloud and lochshore was a multi-coloured throng of climbers so close together that they looked like a technicolour gully. I cannot understand what makes climbers shout to each other in such a place. Is it because they find the landscape so intimidating that they must shout down the intensity of its silences or the sough of its winds? The Cuillin are loud today. My hopes of soft-shoeing over the ridge quiet and alone were thwarted by this bus-party-sized gaggle of loudmouths. From where I sat I could see twelve purple rucksacks, one that was blue, red and yellow, two pink and one pink and lime green, and six orange jackets, four tomato-soup jackets, and not one climber whose gear remotely resembled the colour of the surroundings, unless you count the discreet early flowers of the purple saxifrage, lurking coyly on a ledge, but there was not much coy lurking going on up the mountain. This is not a sulk because I did not have the mountain to myself. It is a protest against climbing disrespectfully. I watched the vivid cavalcade feeling like a dinosaur stranded out of my era. Quiet, even in the mountains, becomes ever more elusive, and I remembered again that one truly intense silence I encountered with David Craig on the Moine Mhor of the Cairngorms, but all I can remember of it is that it happened. Alas, although you can recall voices, music, birdsong, in your mind and reconstruct the sound, you cannot reconvene a silence.

I read Seton Gordon's pages. All the life he had encountered between Glen Brittle and the corrie had been a blue hare and some meadow pipits, and a wren's nest 'unexpectedly at a height of 1700 feet above sea level', and at that my mind was dragged back to the Cairngorms where I found a wren's nest at 2000 feet and conjectured that as there are eagles nesting in pine trees at 1500 feet, here was a wren accustomed to looking-down on the backs of homing eagles. How much truer in the Cuillin where golden eagles (and doubtless sea eagles before too long) cliff-nest much nearer to sea level. It is a bewildering blur, a mountain wren, with ideas above its station and the energy and workaday courage to put them into practice. And if this daunting rock arena of Coir' a Ghrunnda looks too unforgiving and inhospitable for such a bird-mite, I recommend an ocean voyage to the height of incredulity. In a different book about a different island I wrote:

> Long after you learn not to be astonished at St Kilda's unlimited capacity to astonish, you will be astounded at the places you encounter wrens, at the free flow of sweet song, at its power to lift, however fleetingly, even the pervasive mood of hodden-gray gloom with which St Kilda frequently garbs itself for days at a time. On such a day as this there is nothing to dispel but the joysong is a heady embellishment. He sings from the topmost rock of the highest pinnacle of a 50-feet stac three-quarters of the way up Conachair's 1200-feet cliffs. In St Kilda's tumultuous landscape, wrens are nothing daunted.

In the Cuillin too. The way it sometimes happens in wild places, with my thoughts wrapped in wrens and my eyes looking at nothing, a rock snapped into focus with a wren on it, singing, 2400-and-something feet up in the Skye Cuillin, and that song which gladdens your garden and outlived the St Kildans on their ocean rock, sits as easily on the high Cuillin as rainclouds. Suddenly the song shut-down, the wren blurred over the hurdle of the corrie rim and dived down the mountain, perhaps to a nest at 1700 feet. Funny you should mention wrens, Seton.

The mountain wall had finally emptied of its colour-clash climbers, but had begun to fill with cloud, and the weather forecast was in shreds. The wisdom of the whole venture was now called into question, for I wanted Seton Gordon's island panoramas and mackerel skies and moonlight, but it was only a few hundred feet to the bealach and I could reconsider my options there.

The Bealach a' Gharbh-choire, or something vaguely like it, windless cloud clamped down on to its ridge . . . enough to dampen the enthusiasm of any mountaineering ambition. I peered hopefully in every direction including up and down, but here there was not even a wren to put a chink in the gloom. I stood immobile as a rock pinnacle and tried to root myself on the ridge to prise a sense of being out of the mountain element. There are times when it works, in extremes of comfort or discomfort and you feel ancient as pine or cold as granite. But a voice said 'You okay, mate?' and four orange jackets crunched past, and at my reassurance they were gone back into the cloud leaving their voices on the air like a trawler's wake. I consulted the maestro:

> It was evening when I stood on the pass at the head of Coir' a'Ghrunnda. Forty miles westward the cloud canopy ended and Barra showed in orange light . . .

Forty miles! And which was westward?! Forty yards would be a generous assessment of the day's visibility and the only orange shades had been those upwardly mobile jackets. What else should I be seeing, maestro?

> Loch Coruisk, 2700 feet beneath me was already in twilight, and the Garbh-choire a place of gloom . . .

Down then, for gloom and twilight seemed an altogether brighter prospect than this. But remember . . .

> The walk down the Garbh-choire seemed unending.

No, not unending, longer than that, rock in all its forms and gray-black in all its shades, bouldered and broken and tumbling into cloud-shrouded oblivions.

Then, through the wet candy-floss of air, the shadow of wings, beating wheezily and fast, accompanying a hoarse honking-croak. I know that voice, but not up here . . . think. Sound and shadow receded then re-emerged, the bird obviously circling the high corrie, but still I could neither see it nor put a face or a name to the sound. Three times it came close and went flying not far above my head, but the fourth circle was lower and it suddenly cleaved the cloud apart yards ahead, a smooth and hunch-backed shape the same gloom-gray as the mountain and the sky. As it swerved away from the sudden apparition of my stumbling shape, there was a vivid hint of crimson — a red-throated diver. Three more times the bird flew close, one red eye on me as it passed, then on a new and confident course it vanished and the croaking grew distant and feeble and finally beyond reach. It was while I was pondering why the bird should be 2500 feet up a mountain with a cloud ceiling only a few hundred feet lower that I put myself in the bird's position and wondered instead what it would make of my presence there. I asked it aloud: 'Whose footsteps are you following?' But it was gone and I was alone in the Garbh-choire of the Skye Cuillin and I had a mission to accomplish that had begun to take on the aura of a fool's errand. I pushed on down through the cloud, *feeling* the corrie begin to broaden out as I went, and because the mountain mind is at its most restlessly troubled when it has nothing to see and hear, I began to turn the questions I was asking of the diver on to myself. What was *I* doing here? What *was* the point? What was I achieving, stymied halfway between the Corrie

Loch Coir' a Ghrunnda, 2500 feet up in the Skye Cuillin . . . the only thing clearer than its water is its air . . .'

'I cannot look at mist in the Cuillin of Skye and see just mist . . .'

of Earth and the Corrie of Waters by the Rough Corrie and the suffocating porridge of its air?

I piled it on, questioning all the accumulated years of experience which had still not prevented me from walking down one of the toughest pieces of mountainside anywhere in zero visibility towards the near certainty of a cold and uncomfortable night on the lochside, so that I could climb back up again a few hours from now, by which time the cloud will probably have slithered a few hundred feet lower.

I was not worried. I was sure of my position, in the correct corrie going in the correct direction, which was down. All that was beyond reasonable doubt. But I was also on the verge of that realm of unreasonable doubt which the mountain depths can induce when they have a target at their mercy. My line of attack was that I should have had sense enough to turn back on the other side of the bealach in the face of the lowering cloud in the Cuillin of all places and climbing alone of all things. But at that point, I recognised the attack, for it is a familiar predicament when things go wrong and my predeliction for going alone becomes my favourite excuse for my plight. Of course, when it all goes wonderfully well, I take full credit and solitude is the key which unlocks the mountains' resistance. So the attack is turned back on itself, and so it goes, and doubtless for as long as I am up to the psychology of being alone among mountains, that is the way I will prefer to go.

With the warring still unresolved, as it always is, I stepped abruptly out of the cloud and found the reassuring milk-white length of Loch Coruisk far below. Reassuring. I look at the word on the page and it does not begin to do justice to the service Loch Coruisk rendered in that moment. My wayward scheme was thrown a lifejacket, and the craft in which I had voyaged across that mountainous wave of gabbro had at once a reliable anchor and safe haven. You cannot hug a loch, but I sent a notional gesture of deepest affection spinning downhill before me like an avalanche, and settled the voice of my instincts back into my brain from which it had been ousted some time ago. Instinct had taken a more certain assessment of my situation than my brain had. Instinct had concluded that, deprived of the true marvels of the Cuillin — the almost limitless scope of sea and island spread across a vast westward horizon, and the mountains' own island-ness — my trek would turn in on itself the way the Cuillin do. Instinct saw danger in the gray shroud and my unfamiliarity with the bealach and the Garbh-choire, questioned the wisdom of crossing my self-styled rubicon, and my brain had shouted it down.

Now, the dilemma shelved if not resolved, I went gleefully down into the corrie's depths and I heard a song spill from a mouth that had none of the assurance of my own: a half-whispered air, *Women of Skye*, which once it had escaped from me seemed to hang on the still air on its arrangement of notes. I listened to my barely audible self and puzzled over an underpinning layer of sound. In the lower Garbh-choire, a great depth of Cuillin is revealed, from Sgurr nan Gillean in the north to Bla Bheinn in the east, but within that compass-arc are the serried ranks of lesser gabbro upheavals, small mountains, ridges, glens, lochs and outcrops. In the flat and dusky light, these stood apart from each other and were elevated in their solitary stature while the great landmark peaks were pulled down into their mass, undistinguished by a different light or a snow crown or (in the summit-smothering cloud) a mighty silhouette. The Munro-bagger differentiates among the Cuillin and by-passes the lower echelons. Yet Sgur na Stri and Druim na Ramh and Strath na Creithach, for example, are pieces of the same jigsaw puzzle of dowsed fire and melted ice, no less Cuillin, and in some lights and some states of mind, just as crucial to the completeness of the mountain mass. Norman MacCaig was right, but he always had a shrewd eye for a landscape as well as a poet's gifts. And as my small song and the burn's amicable accompaniment swilled about in the air of the Garbh-choire, I recognised that sound which underpinned them; it was that singular 'intense silence' in which a dark mass of gabbro dwells forever when it has come to rest.

The Garbh-choire goes on forever, an eternity of downhill which turns knees to soap. I would not have believed there was a foreground in the land which could have kept my eyes lowered in the face of Bla Bheinn, but such are the underfoot treacheries of the corrie that I could look on my most beloved of all island mountains only by standing still. I stopped often, for even snooded in cloud, the long south ridge of Bla Bheinn is my first highway of the Skye Cuillin in any light. Even Seton Gordon found the corrie a trial:

> To descend it is a toil and a weariness . . .

They relent, these treacheries, not far above the loch and among deep heather. Seton Gordon made a fire here with dried rowan wood, but there was not so much as a stick for me. Besides, I had packed a small stove and two ancient pans which have done almost as many mountain miles with me as my feet. Coffee and bacon and eggs on the still shore of Loch Coruisk entombed by darkening, closing Cuillin walls, having laboured and agonised for the privilege . . . only bog myrtle smells better. A hip-flask swig of Talisker (which being the Skye malt was as sweet here as the mountain air!) made a passable liqueur, and I stretched out in dry-ish heather to rest and doze and look at the dusk mountains lying on my back. Five contemplative minutes, then . . .
  'Knock three times on the ceiling
  if you wa-han' me!!!'
Oh shit. The bus party.
  They were gathered in the gloom of the top end of the loch and apparently getting drunk. I considered the valour of protest, opted for discretion, stashed the stove, washed the pans, shouldered the pack and sauntered off down the loch towards the ocean where it digs deep into south Skye in the guise of Loch Scavaig. I would put distance between me and the bus party, but it was also part of the expedition. Seton Gordon had walked that way to see the full moon rise in the south: he saw it 'orange, full-orbed and majestic', then, '. . . she shone serenely upon a silent sleeping world of unusual beauty . . .'

I had neither orb nor silence, but the beauty was unquestionably unusual. The moon lit the thick matt of cloud from above so that it paled and spread about the ridges like a second sea 2000 feet higher than the one which slapped at my feet. The great Cuillin prow, Gars-bheinn, sliced down through both seas, an unbroken diagonal which at once recalled the sun in Sannox, so sharply did it bisect the shades of mountain and island sky into dark black and pale black. In daylight, the mountain's unstoppable and perfect profile is never less than impressive. By this suggestive half darkness and with its summit sheered off by the palest of night clouds, it was unforgettable, an unfathomable blackness. But the way it emerged from the cloud sea invited the idea of that same singular mountain sweep diving headlong and deep under Loch Scavaig, down and darkly down for miles, until far, far down, the foundations of Gars-bheinn and the offshore island of Soay fuse in the same sunken land bridge. The basking sharks which once played such a crucial role in the economic well-being of Soay when Gavin Maxwell was its laird would have had a perspective of Gars-bheinn beyond the scope of mere mortals for they would dive as deep as the mountain. To see mountain and island forge their age-old link . . . that would be to redefine my ideas about the depth of mountains, but on the dark Scavaig shore, I came closer to understanding its meaning than I am ever likely to again, and did so by the light of a moon which never shone.

It was two a.m. when I wandered back up the lochside and prepared to sit out the last of the brief night. The bus party appeared to have gone comatose under a small mushrooming of flimsy mist. Seton Gordon saw that mist.

> Can it have been the magic mist in which the nymph of Loch Coruisk conceals herself — that nymph 'who comes there only when she knows that someone is present who will love her'? Beside the loch, in the silence of the night, she sings and weaves beautifully, but never a word must one say to her.

That was no nymph I heard singing. It is a different spirit which the modern climber takes with him on to the night shore of Coruisk than such as Seton Gordon, carrying with him his store of Celtic myths and half believing perhaps in his 'affinity with the world of dreams and visions'.

I dozed, but mostly I just lay still and wondered at the devil within me that egged me on into such situations alone and far from home and loved ones. But I had to concede that at that moment (between my bouts with the Garbh-choire), and in a state of ease and repose, something elemental was put into place like a well-fitted lock closing. Something indefinable in me meshed utterly with my surroundings, and a sense of one-ness with the wildest of mountain shores was briefly mine. That is all. No summit is higher. There *is* nothing higher, no greater reward or purpose, not among

PREVIOUS PAGE:
Bla Bheinn is the matchless backdrop for one more spectacular show of Skye's island light

146

mountains, any mountains anywhere, for it is as if I have become, fleetingly, of the mountain itself, shared the sense of permanence it knows. I have tasted it more than once, and it was the memory of its savour, bitter-sweet on the tongue and the throat, which had brought me here, and would again some wild somewhere or other. But the savour grows daily – and nightly – more elusive.

A gull called from one of the islands on the loch, and I sat up to watch it stir. The sky lightened, I had slept all I would sleep, the bus party was lost beneath the mist of the nymph. It was five a.m. I thrust my head into the burn by way of a wakening wash while the coffee boiled. I packed and stood, and sipping as I walked the first easy reaches I pushed myself back into the Garbh-choire. I climbed it dull and numb, the price of the mountain's revealed secrets.

As the corrie steepened and narrowed over an eternity of wearying, foot-burning, hand-scraping hours (gabbro is wondrously adhesive but a raw taskmaster on human extremities) I began to focus my mind on that pivotal moment when I would cross the rubicon again, see again the instantly materialised world beyond the Cuillin, beyond Skye. Surely the cloud was rising, surely the ridge was clearing, surely the panorama of sea and islands was unfolding even now, unseen by me yet but preparing itself. Seton Gordon knew the moment:

On the instant a glorious view south-west and south opened out . . .

On the instant, I walked into a wall of rising cloud which had Coir' a' Ghrunnda by the throat.

I crossed and went down into the new depths without pausing, but there was less than a moment for disappointment for the Cuillin threw one more startling sensation at me. The instant I stepped across over the rim of Coir' a' Ghrunnda, 2700 feet up, I was hit full in the face by the smell of the sea, and more forcibly than any panorama of oceans could ever have impressed me, I recognised one more uncanny symptom of that magical realm among mountains among islands.

I mourn the passing of the Seton Gordons of this land. He loved and was fluently versed in the mountain landscape, its wildlife, its people, its myths, its music. It is one thing to take your pipes with you and play a pibroch on the evening shores of Coruisk, for such music is born of such a landscape. It is another to get drunk and sing pop songs. One is the response of a man who knew the three dimensions of the mountain, and was well versed in a fourth, that fey Celtic perception of places set apart. The other is the response of an ever more prevalent thoughtlessness which in terms of mountain dimensions is satisfied by two at the most, possibly less.

I had the late morning to myself on the shore of Loch Coir' a' Ghrunnda, the sun full on the Cuillin, the clouds shrivelling, and the weather catching up with the forecast for the day before. But I had Seton Gordon's eloquent word for such a day and such a night of still and clear skies and orbed moons and intense silence, and I had my own day and night to set against it in my own time which is all but beyond silence, beyond that time when a celebrated man of the mountains could still write:

> Eager breezes more than once ruffled the calm surface of Loch Coir' a' Ghrunnda. They were the herdsmen of the mists, and since the mists were lost to them they crossed the lochan aimlessly, as the clan of dreams that take their departure at sunrise.

But I, for one, cannot look at mist in the Cuillin of Skye and see just mist.

Chapter Twelve

AMONG MOUNTAINS

IT IS THE end of summer in the mountains. The air is unclear, familiar mountain profiles grow hazily vague and wear unaccustomed green. Distance and depth grow uncertain. The skin of the mountain wrinkles wretchedly under the throb of too many boots, the jaws of too many sheep, too many deer. Guns go after grouse and the shutters on shooting lodges creak open and let in the stranger sun. Old boys hark back and that grizzled old euphemism, 'sporting estate' embarks on one more orgy of self-indulgence. I stay away and ache for autumn.

I sit on a lochside well known to me for half my life where the young ospreys practise and grow strong. They have little enough time for fishing skills to be honed, for wings to gain the fluency which will carry them to Africa. Two more weeks and they will be gone. A young bird crosses the woody shore and begins a strafing run across the watersheet, 'bouncing' a dozen times across the water like a Barnes Wallis bomb, climbs, spirals twice, hovers inexpertly, hugs its wings close, tips forward, falls, throws its wings high as an archangel, smashes the water feet first then stops. The water subsides. The wings are flat on the water, the head and chest bobbing like a lobster float, the snared trout an unco-operative prey and trying desperately to dive down. Seconds pass. On the shore, I will the osprey to do something. My bottom lip is in the grip of my top teeth. Fly for God's sake. Twenty seconds, and still the bird is floating. I try to imagine the small underwater war as the talons try to improve their grip, the trout tries to unhook. Twenty-five seconds and the wings lift a few inches and slap down. Nothing. Thirty seconds and the bird tries again. It is not that it has caught a five-pounder: it is just that it has caught something, and doesn't know what to do next. The bird knows it should be flying, that the fish is in its element and the bird is not. Three vast slapping wingbeats pull its chest up. Three more and there is space under the trailing feet. The fish is hooked on one talon of one foot, and struggling. It does not like flying. The fish falls free from perhaps ten feet above the water, but its splash is shadowed by great wings. The osprey has wheeled and folded and thrust and fallen and glided down to snatch it back from the surface, and the Barnes Wallis bombing run practice has paid off, perfectly. This time the bird is high and away to a pine tree where the bark is bruised and bloodied and generations of trout have died.

As the bird flies across my field of vision and I follow him in the field-glasses, he crosses a handsome mountain profile. The mountain dominates utterly the loch's north-west corner, a long, smooth, elegant shape which is in itself part of the pleasure of the lochshore. I have watched almost twenty generations of ospreys against that mountain shape. Through more than eighty seasons I have seen it whiten and darken, grow green, and burnish in autumn. There are days when it looks as forbidding as Everest, others when it's as benign as a hillock. There are days when storm clouds obliterate its presence, bit by bit, and when it re-emerges it has changed colour. It is black, white, gray, blue, green, brown, gold, yellow, purple, lilac. There are days, too, when the wind shifts, pulls down a brightly impenetrable summer haze and removes the mountain entirely. On such a late summer day, how I envy the mountain from my lochshore!

> That wind that moves mountains
> blew my way today,
> blew my mountain away
>
> from its accustomed shore, deftly
> rearranging a million tons
> of granite. Silkscreens
>
> of summer haze smuggled it
> out of my country.
> Sometimes I sit shorebound wishing
>
> that wind, that mountain-mover,
> would billow and blow by
> when I perch eagle-high instead
>
> so that mountain and I
> might try a new season
> out of our country.
>
> I'm sure mountain and I
> together, granitic kin,
> could sweet-talk that wind
>
> to thumb us a lift
> with a passing mistral.
> Our desultory destinies would align

on a kind and unaccustomed shore
where I might part silkscreens
of an old summer and find

the bright burnished mountain
of a new autumn.

It seems to me that my native mountain landscape stagnates under the burdensome oppression of an old summer. Conservation thinking has mostly grown moribund and dull. Land *use* is all but extinct. Only land abuse thrives. Those social and economic dinosaurs we call sporting estates still hold vastnesses of mountains in straitjackets which inhibit any form of natural vigour. With very few praiseworthy exceptions, landowners preoccupy themselves with the stale economics of their trade. Imagination is not a tool of that trade, and to talk of reform in their earshot is to invite accusations of anarchy, treachery and worse. Yet few things are more certain in our mountain landscapes than the need for reform of land ownership.

The deer forest is done. The Highlander has always treated it with something between resentment and polite contempt. It did as much as anything to drive him off his land and it perpetuates a class system which is now no more than a propped up and crumbling facade. The changing climate of public opinion has shifted to such an extent that an organisation such as the John Muir Trust can come into being dedicated to owning land, restoring indigenous habitat *and* sustaining the native population. The only reason that they have proved successful already (albeit in a limited way as yet) where others have not is because they have tried and others have not and it is as simple as that. Of course it is workable. It is how the Highlands lived throughout their history before the sporting estate was invented.

The days of monoculture forest are numbered. The landowner's soft option has reached too many saturation points and attracted too many salvoes of public indignation. The Highland hill farm has reached its most marginal subsidised extreme while the next most degrading land use for mountains is tourism which has dwindled in the face of recessions and poor weather. There is a better way.

It is to turn our entire mountain landscape over to the one growth industry which is sustainable for all time, even in the Highlands. It does not rely on the weather, it is immune to boom and recession, it is not seasonal, it requires new and traditional skills and training, it is labour intensive, and more importantly than all these considerations put together, it accords the mountain landscape its due. It is that species of conservation on the grand scale which Aldo Leopold called 'cures'. It requires the commitment of our own people, and therefore of the government, so it requires a Scottish parliament in the first place, for no Westminster government will unpick the last threads of a landowning system with which it is inextricably interwoven. But, for the sake of furthering the argument, say the following reforms were implemented in a

'The mountain dominates utterly the loch's north-western corner . . . I have watched it for more than eighty seasons . . .'

Crofting is a key element in the return to health of our mountain landscape and the Highland population

ten-year introduction programme dedicated to the return to health of our mountain landscape *and* the Highland population:

* No individual to own more than 10,000 acres.
* No organisation to own more than 10,000 acres without a track record and a declared and detailed intention to manage with conservation as the first priority.
* No land to be owned, developed or grazed above 2000 feet.
* Restoration and replanting of native forests on a scale at least commensurate with commercial forests.
* Relief from overgrazing of mountains by sheep and deer: culls in some places by as much as three-quarters of the population and the eventual restoration of the red deer to its true place in the mountain landscape as a woodland animal, and the sheep to its true place in the mountain landscape – oblivion.
* Widespread expansion of crofting.

The mountains are the ultimate realm of wild nature. Nature barely recognises us there now, we are such strangers. The mountains are the last strongholds, the deepest refuges, of nature. The only unnatural threats to stronghold and refuge are the ones we pose. Nature *needs* the mountains. We do not, although we can benefit greatly from a respectful association with them.

The world stirs to the summoning of its environmental conscience. We stir with it. We berate the fellers of tropical rainforests, the despoilers of polar wilderness, the slayers of whales, the puncturers of the ozone layer. But who should heed us, we who preside over the near extinction of our native pine forest; we who poison our own eagles; we who strangle our own mountains?

Yet we, the race of people we call Scots, *are* the mountains. Their landscape is what others judge us by, and whether we think of ourselves as Highlander or Lowlander or Islander or something else, we all look to them as the unyielding granite in the backbone of our nation. We are shaped by them. They have given us our stoicism, our reputation for hospitable shelter, our temperament of storms.

They have in the past inspired and sustained that Celtic element in us which is our most dignified and sophisticated civilisation. They could do so again. Nothing will assist their cause so readily as increasing our own living presence in their midst so long as it is an understanding, sympathetic, proud, native presence willing and eager to renew the ancient bond.

The mountains are nature's enlightenment. They are her greatest works. They are the substance where dwells the clan of dreams, and if we can only learn to revere them again, they would ennoble and enlighten us too. Blow, wind. Blow our mountains a new autumn.

The Empty Glen

A thousand technicolour climbers cried
'The Wilderness, the Great Outdoors!'
and laughed delight while I wept
for wildness and greatness swept
to the far mouth of the sea glen.
Colour and tilth withered here
with people and song
(these now belong

to a vile chronicle
whose ripples widen still).
This glen was whittled back,
whittled back, brittled black

until it snapped
under a brutal bondage.
Only the divers and I return.
We alone mourn.

Drab deer and shoddy sheep
stripped wilderness of finery,
browsed the glen to the bone
– the flesh is gone,

save that eagle overlords
eke out taloned revenge
for the glen's long sleep
on winter-weary deer, slip-shoddy sheep.

Yet still the empty glen compels
and whiles dispels my melancholy
(old lichened lintel stone
is fit tribute for what is gone)

and still phlegmatic bens
preach unimpeachable wisdoms,

don and doff their snows
in season. No weakness shows

this high, this mighty. Here
hope springs and sings
eternal meltwater-pure
— I drink — and sure

of the destiny of this
cold and empty glen, I urge
some slumbering God-of-the-wild
to one more new-born mountain child.

BIBLIOGRAPHY

CAMPBELL, Marion, *Argyll, The Enduring Heartland*; Turnstone Press, 1977

CRAIG, David, *Native Stones*; Secker and Warburg, 1987, Fontana Paperbacks, 1988
    On the Crofters' Trail; Jonathan Cape, 1990

CRUMLEY, Jim, *A High and Lonely Place*; Jonathan Cape, 1991
    with BAXTER, Colin, *Glencoe, Monarch of Glens*; Baxter, 1990
    St Kilda; Baxter, 1988
    West Highland Landscape; Baxter, 1989

GORDON, Seton, *The Cairngorm Hills of Scotland*; Cassell, 1925
    The Charm of Skye; Cassell, 1929

LEOPOLD, Aldo, *A Sand County Almanac*; Oxford University Press, 1947

MACCAIG, Norman, *Collected Poems*; Chatto & Windus, 1985

MAXWELL, Gavin, *Harpoon at a Venture*; Hart-Davis, 1952
    Ring of Bright Water; Longmans Green, 1960

SCROGGIE, Syd, *Give Me the Hills*; David Winter, 1978

TOMKIES, Mike, *Golden Eagle Years*; Heinemann, 1982
    Last Wild Years; Jonathan Cape, 1992